RIDING WITH ROY

SINCLAIR CURRIE

Published by Watson Ferguson & Company
an imprint of Boolarong Press
38/1631 Wynnum Road
Tingalpa Qld 4173
Australia.
www.boolarongpress.com.au

First published 2020

A catalogue record for this book is available from the National Library of Australia

ISBN: 9780648484233 (paperback)

Cover design by Ailsa Currie

Printed and bound by Watson Ferguson & Company, Tingalpa, Australia

To Roy and Boyd

who continue to push me up life's hills.

INTRODUCTION

This species of book is best filed under the general heading of Retirement Planning. If that description immediately makes you imagine a book filled with advice about how to make money last in retirement, then it isn't that sort of book. This is about retirement planning of the physical kind. Its pages deal, directly or indirectly, with what actions you might need to take in order to stay healthy and have an ongoing quality of life into old age. Naturally, health and wellbeing are much more important than financial wellbeing, so proper planning for the physical body is something absolutely everyone should address as they age.

On one level, this is a book which merely explores the inevitable consequences of aging bodies deciding to ride bikes. However, this is only a mechanism for examining the underlying message — that physical health, and in particular heart health, are the main drivers of a good quality old age. Read it as deeply or as superficially as you wish. On one level, it can be read as a book of humour and of cautionary tales of the old riding their bikes and behaving as if they were young again. But threaded through it is information that allows you to understand exactly what happens to your heart and body when you exercise. It might sometimes wear a clown hat, and sidle up to the subject obliquely. But in essence, it is a book designed to make you think about how you might approach old age so that you have both quality as well as longevity to your life.

As a book, it began its life as a collection of humorous short stories documenting the predictable misadventures flowing from old men riding bikes; a book whose purpose was to entertain, and be merely a celebration of growing old, disgracefully. Within the humour, though, was always an intent to present an alternative vision of what old age might look like, no matter how skewed and 'out there' that vision might be.

However, it soon became evident this was only half the story. The other half was the beneficial physical changes that come with exercise. The story became, not just about the fun that could still be had in old age, but also about the resulting enduring improvement to the body, and in particular to the heart and blood vessels. Slowly and inevitably it morphed into a book about heart health, and its central position in proper retirement planning. It became a book with a message, and the messages of the book can be summarised: we should not drift into old age with no plan for our continuing physical wellbeing, and the necessary starting point of smart retirement planning for the body is in having a healthy heart.

As it happens, I found myself equipped to tell both parts of the story; the first because it was merely a first-hand account of my own journey, and the second part, because I possessed the required understanding of the physiology of the cardiovascular system due to my professional background in imaging hearts and blood vessels. I use the slow journey from couch potato to enthusiastic bike rider to illustrate the gradual changes that occur to hearts, blood vessels, and the rest of the body, once we start to exercise. I also explain the 'whys' of the adverse changes occurring to those who choose to remain sedentary.

Naturally, we'd all like our hearts to stay healthy, but as with most things in life, wishful thinking is not enough. This book enables you to form a working understanding of how hearts become unhealthy, the processes involved in heart arteries becoming diseased, and why a sedentary lifestyle has a negative impact on the quality of heart muscle. It also explains why exercise positively impacts heart muscle health, and why that matters. There should be no argument that these are understandings worth gaining; after all, without exception, we all have a stake in the heart-health game.

I've kept the important educational sections on hearts, short, and most of the text is given over to tall but true tales of misadventure. Hopefully, these stories of old men riding their bikes will entertain, but also challenge commonly-held views about the capabilities of aging bodies. Hopefully, it will also give you confidence that even high-grade exercise is something not to be scared of in middle and old-age. I hope reading it will do your heart good on many levels.

BEGINNINGS

I SIT IN THE SHOWER WITH MY HEAD BETWEEN MY KNEES, AND wait for the distress in my chest and arms to subside. Every so often, I take in a deep breath and sigh. I should be dressing for work, but my heart is still racing, my pulse thready. The blood that should be going to my head evidently is being routed elsewhere, leaving me light and strangely fuzzy. I let the warm water spill down the back of my head until the thick waves of discomfort slowly subside. Right at this moment, I'm thinking this bike riding business is a mistake, and much more likely to kill me, than ever do me any good.

Yet even as I sit here feeling grey and pasty, I still sense I've been thrown a lifeline, and I had better take hold of it with both hands. The hard, inescapable truth is that I'm overweight and unfit, caught in an unfortunate spiral of lessening mobility reducing participation, and lessening participation further reducing mobility. My fifty-year-old body is already adrift on the upper slopes of a long slide, which will all too soon deliver me to the inevitability of a shuffling old age. What's more, I sense that if I don't jump right now and grab that lifeline, the outcomes will inexorably take on the fixed tragic proportions of irreversibility.

My wife already points out that, whenever I bend down to pick anything up, I grunt like an old man. Putting socks on has become a major, straining, red-faced exercise. I roll out of bed in the morning and limp my painful way around till my joints warm up. My puffing, token, ever more infrequent runs along the beach have been reduced to a combination of walk, and a slow embarrassing shuffle. What's more, I'm in denial, imagining I'm only large around the middle; the pregnant stomach spreading out across the bed, surely more about lax abdominal muscles than fat. After all, as I point out in the most pathetic denial of them all, there are plenty who are in much worse shape than I am. At least I still occasionally try to exercise, but a bad back over the last few years has become an all-purpose rationale for a life of ever-decreasing activity. Sport is now something to be watched. With 'used to' attached to the many enjoyable physical activities now consigned to the past. Like many others, I'm heading, docile and accepting, into a sedentary, complaining, shortened old age.

That I am sitting in this shower feeling like death warmed up is down to my friend Roy. As you will soon come to understand, Roy is an endlessly optimistic force of nature, whose enthusiasms are many and infectious. In my case, while he has had to be persistent and relentlessly cajoling, his gentle bullying has finally pushed me off the couch. With my body complaining its rear-guard objections, he's deposited me reluctantly onto a pushbike. Of course, had I known at that time what Roy's grand plan entailed — if he'd laid out the big picture in all its pain and sweaty impossibility, rather than reveal each tiny incremental attainable step at a time — would I ever have thrown my leg over that bike? Looking back from here, I hope I would have. But, if I'd known it all from the beginning, I'd certainly have laughed, and then I'd have sat down and cried.

The suggestion comes out of left field and catches me by surprise. "But, Roy, I don't even own a bike," I say, pointing out the obvious difficulty. "I used to have an old road bike when the kids were young, but I can't remember what happened to it. It would be over twenty years since I last even sat on a bike seat."

"No problem," Roy insists, dismissing the difficulty with a mere flick of the hand. "The thing about riding a bike is that it's like riding a bike — you never forget how, and if you want to come riding, I'll find you a bike."

While I don't want to disappoint him, all I can see are the problems. "Bouncing my back up and down on a bike seat? I don't know about that. It hurts enough already."

"Listen, riding is absolutely all low impact stuff," he says with his relentless enthusiasm. "No stress on the joints — no strain on the back. If you can't run or do other stuff because of the back thing, this will be perfect for you." I'm now regretting admitting my lack of fitness to him, and in my mind I'm firming my resistance at being steamrolled. But then he says the fateful words. "And, anyway, your heart needs to do this." And there it was — half a dozen simple words arrowing straight through laziness, objections, and my fatal ambivalence, to instantly skewer all defences: "Your heart needs to do this." As these few words reverberate in my head, I hear a bell tolling for me. I know I'm looking at a forked road, and what I glimpse down one of the paths scares me. With life-changing clarity, I realise I need to make a choice, and that choice needs to be 'change'. "I'll go down to the bike shop tomorrow, and see what I can find," I say without enthusiasm. Naively, I think I've finally bitten the bullet and merely decided to buy a bicycle to enjoy the health benefits of exercise. I've no inkling that what I've really done, is take the first tentative step down a long and winding road that will deliver me to Roy's decidedly alternative vision of growing old.

Common sense walks me straight past the skinny tyres of the sleek racers at the front of the bike shop. A helpful assistant asks, "What sort of bike are you looking for?"

"A bike I can't fall off," I reply.

He laughs, but I'm not being funny.

"Comfortable, too," I add as another essential requirement.

He directs me to the section where the tyres are thick, the handlebars high, the seats wide. I sit on an array of shiny machines, while he talks of combinations of cogs and clusters, and gushes over the quality of derailleurs and running gear. It all washes over my head as I move from bike to bike, sitting on each seat till I find a bike that feels 'just right.' It has tyres that are thick enough to allow me to feel stable and secure, and wide flat handlebars that let me sit high and comfortable. So, seduced by its bright orange colour and seemingly endless combinations of gears, and with the enthusiastic assurances from the store's owner that this bike is perfect for me, I leave the shop the proud owner of my first ever new bicycle.

I decide to ride to work a few days a week. It's ten kilometres there, and ten back; surely anyone can ride ten kilometres. The route takes me through a patch of coastal rainforest, on into an orchard, across cane fields and finally onto bitumen for the rest of the way. There are a few small hills — the kind that when you drive them in a car, are hard to even recall as hills. Each day I set off full of hope and optimism, and each day delivers the same blow to my tenuous enthusiasm. The flatlands are quiet and pleasant, and I enjoy the fresh air. Then comes the first hill. I always seem to start well, and with an optimism that this time things will be different. Gently sloping to begin with, the hill lulls and deceives, until halfway to the top the slope kicks up slightly, and I begin to crunch the unfamiliar gears ever lower. The front tyre begins to wobble, my breathing to labour, and the glances I throw up the road become more frequent and ever more desperate. Unfortunately, the slope is steepest towards the top. While the 'need to stop' signals begin to flash urgently inside my head, I feel myself move into the chest-tightening, head-bursting discomfort of oxygen debt. Each day, I force myself to the crest of the hill, I stop, my head drops towards the handlebars and my chest heaves. When recovered enough, I have a long slow drink and let my distressed breathing settle. I can't believe how unfit I am. Looking back down the hill, I once again register how relatively gentle the slope is, and yet I'm struggling. How could I let myself get this way? Only two more hills to go, I tell myself, and I move off to repeat the experience.

For two or three weeks, there is no change in the familiar pattern. I struggle up the last hill to work, and when I hop off my legs are jelly, my body is suffused by a vague, unnamed distress. I stay light, and not quite myself, till about lunchtime, then after a few hours of feeling normal, I again face the struggle home. I make it to my front gate, walk slowly up the stairs, throw myself onto the bed, and lie motionless for an hour. At night I fall asleep with my pulse still fast, and vaguely fearful that my heart will say, "Enough of this nonsense", and stop.

Roy rings me up, and I find I'm looking forward to the conversation. Geography separates us, so he's ignorant of my progress. While I wait for him to ask the question, we talk about work and family, and all the usual subjects.

"Been on that new bike yet?" he finally asks.

"Yes," I say with a casualness that's hard to maintain. "Been riding to work two or three times a week for the last three weeks. Of course, It's only ten Ks," I quickly add, keen to downplay the achievement, "but it's something, at least."

"No, that's great. That's really, really, good," he enthuses as if I'd just claimed I'd run a marathon in world record time.

"I don't know if it's doing me that much good, though," I confess. "The hills just aren't getting any easier. I think maybe I'm just getting too old for serious exertion."

"No, listen, you've just got to keep at it," he cuts in with unbridled passion, as if a star recruit was threatening to give the game away. "See, at the moment, your body is still in the process of adjusting to what you're asking it to do and hasn't quite got the message that this is stuff you now do every day. Once it works that out, then it'll start to make the good changes. Right now, it's still rearranging the furniture, and everything's complaining, but if you just keep going, your heart and body will respond. Good stuff will begin to happen."

"Good stuff, like, what?" I ask.

"You'll know it when it happens … You'll feel it. You're beginning to get back to using things as they were designed to be used. Keep the effort going, don't let up and, eventually, all the good heart and body stuff will begin to happen for you."

"Or alternatively, my heart will say, 'Enough' and just give up," I joke nervously.

Then one day, I ride up the first hill, and before I realise it, I pedal on without stopping for a 'drink.' The need to linger long in the shower also disappears, as does the strange lightness that used to stay with me all morning. The face that stares back from the mirror as I dress for work is now red from effort, and not a pasty grey. I don't seem to be pedalling up the hills any faster or to be breathing any less hard at the top, but I'm no longer distressed like I was, and the periods of hard breathing are shorter. Then one day it rains heavily, and I feel cheated that I can't ride to work. It's then I realise I've made the transition — I've gone over to the dark side, and become a bike rider.

CHAPTER 1
WETTING THE FEET

MUCH AVAILABLE INFORMATION ON HEART HEALTH AND HEART disease comes in the form of glib, neatly packaged facts. We're informed that smoking, high blood pressure, and diabetes all significantly increase the chances of us suffering a heart attack, or a stroke. We are also continually reminded of the importance of exercise in promoting heart health, and the role of proper diet in reducing the chances of heart disease. However, there is little or no explanation of the actual operative how-and-why mechanisms of heart disease development or prevention. Nobody explains in easily grasped simple terms, why some things increase risk or, conversely, why the exercise we are encouraged to engage in lowers the risk. All we are presented with are bare facts, and unless we are prepared to wade through dense scientific articles, we remain none-the-wiser as far as the important 'how' and 'why' questions are concerned. However, only once there is a good understanding of the causes, then, and only then, will the remedies make sense.

This is not a medical book. It keeps things simple. But, then again, the heart is merely a simple pump, and all you will need is a simple understanding of how it works to grasp the necessary 'how' and 'why'. To make it even simpler, I'll concentrate on how normal hearts become diseased, and avoid anything more complicated.

The preparatory work for this book has already largely been done, as heart disease is so common that most of us have already, directly or indirectly, felt its touch. The non-medical public talk the language of heart attacks and strokes, even if they have no understanding of the content, and everyone already understands that heart disease kills, and cuts many productive lives tragically short. We also know many of those it doesn't kill, suffer a dramatically reduced quality of life. While the miracles of modern medicine might mean that sufferers still live on into their seventies and eighties, the last few decades of that life are often of poor quality; lingering, and miserable.

The first thing to understand about hearts is that the heart is merely a muscle. Just like any other muscle, it responds positively to being worked, and the more we use it, the stronger it becomes and functions more efficiently. Exercise works the heart, and strengthens the heart muscle. It also changes it in other good ways, many of which I will describe in the chapters which follow. Conversely, the less we use it, the weaker it becomes, and the less efficiently it works. This 'use-it-or-lose-it' principle is fundamental, and inbuilt in our bodies. It is one we can readily recognise and easily understand. At its most extreme, we see the leg muscles of people who become paraplegics waste away quickly, because the body recognises they are no longer needed. Even a few months in a plaster cast will see muscle bulk shrink in that limb. The heart muscle might be in continuous use, but the same principle still applies. If we live a lifestyle marked by inactivity, the body will give us the kind of heart that suits that lifestyle. Unfortunately, having weak heart muscle is not the same as having, say, weak flabby arm muscles. Heart muscle is different from other muscles. Heart muscle operates a pump, with the heart's contraction generating the internal pump pressures. The efficiency of that pump depends on the quality and strength of the heart muscle powering it. In ways that I will explain in later chapters, poor quality heart muscle will alter the pressures inside the pump. However, this is not a one-way street, as the changed pressures, in turn, re-impact negatively on the quality of the heart muscle. This can set up a tit-for-tat cycle, where the pressure changes resulting from the poorly-functioning muscle themselves cause further deterioration in that muscle, which then impact on the pressures in an ever cascading cycle. As I will outline in the chapters that follow, a sedentary lifestyle is not without consequences for anyone. Though slow and creeping, if we don't pay attention to heart muscle health as we age, changes happen within the heart which tragically can become permanent and irreversible.

Roy rings up. "There's a ride coming up in a couple of weeks, if you're interested. We'll be driving down towards the New South Wales border, setting up camp beside the creek, and riding out from there, both days." I know there's a difference between riding ten kilometres to work of a morning, and going for a long, all weekend ride, but my response, nevertheless, is an instant 'yes'.

Though it's only been a few months, somewhere in that time I've crossed a psychological line, and begun to feel an addict's craving for wind-in-the-face experiences. Still, I know the body is lagging way far behind where the mind has leapt, and so I ride to work most days in the intervening weeks, in an attempt to minimize the anticipated suffering.

I watch the weather forecast for the weekend with increasing concern. Disappointed, I ring Roy up. "Rain, heavy at times, developing Saturday and extending into Sunday."

"Better bring a raincoat, then," he says as if that was the only issue raised by the weather forecast. "I've got a big tarp," he adds reassuringly. "I'll bring that along, and we can throw it over all the tents, and keep us dry."

I make it down early to Roy's place on the Gold Coast. The weather is clouding over, but holding. As usual, Roy is doing ten things at once, and still has six of them to do by the time I arrive, so it's late morning before we're underway. I don't mind. In theory, a two-day ride should be twice the pleasure of one, but I'd already had feedback from my friend Tony about Roy's two-day rides: "My backside got so sore halfway through the second day, that I had to ring my wife up to come and get me in the car and take me home." I sense that the later we leave, the more my rear end will thank me.

"Big Al's gone up early to get the tents up," Roy says, apologising for not being ready.

Big Al is Roy's brother-in-law. A champion bike rider in his younger days, he's now over sixty years old and twice that in kilograms. Yet, though he lumbers around on land, when he sits on a bike, he still looks the real deal.

The weather is still holding by the time we reach the campground. It is tucked away off the road, on the bank of a creek. To access it we cross the creek, which is gently flowing a few centimetres deep over a concrete causeway. Big Al has already made camp in a pretty spot well away from the dozen other tents clumped together over on the high ground by the creek bank. As usual, Roy is in high spirits at the prospect of fun. By the time we muck around setting up the rest of the tents, with extra attention paid to making ourselves waterproof, the day is slipping away, and there's only time for a relatively short ride. This suits me. Ten kilometres one way and ten back is my comfort zone. We follow a side road which crosses and then re-crosses the shallow waters of the creek. The water spraying up my legs stirs long-submerged memories of something good that's long lost in the fogs of time.

It's as if I've returned to being fifteen again, and it's a grand, welcome feeling. I test myself on a few small hills, and though breathless at the top, I'm recovering well before for the next one comes along. After a few hours, we ride back over the little creek and into the camping ground, and I sense my heart's going to enjoy this weekend on every level.

The rain starts gently enough, and hardly interrupts the fireside chat. Eventually, though, it sets in more heavily, driving us off to bed early, and I enjoy falling asleep to the sound of it slapping on the big tarp covering the tents. Drifting in and out of sleep, I'm aware of the rain becoming steadily heavier, but I'm cosy in the sleeping bag, even if a little uncomfortable sleeping on the bare ground with only a thin mattress underneath. I don't mind how heavily it rains, just as long as it rains itself out, and leaves the coming day dry for the big ride. Somewhere in the middle of the night, though, two things happen simultaneously. I become very cold and at the same time extremely comfortable. I wake up enough to grasp the fact that I'm floating on a cushion of water. I push on the now soft floor of the tent, and feel a rippling layer of water flowing beneath my finger. Something tells me this could be a very bad situation, but at the moment I'm just too comfortable to entertain any worry, and the floor of the tent seems dry, as does my sleeping bag. So I give a sleepy shrug, pull the sleeping bag more tightly around me, roll over and fall back into a cool but very comfortable sleep.

In the morning, it becomes apparent why everyone else had camped over on the high ground. The hillside has funnelled water down into this low area where we are camped, and a shallow stream is flowing under the tents, down on into the creek. We're waterlogged, but Roy is far from miserable. He's in the habit of greeting the gift of each new day with the same outrageous enthusiasm, and this is no exception. I can hear him outside, splashing in the water as if it's one gigantic puddle to play in. I stick my head out of the tent.

"Would you have a look at this," he says, kicking water in my direction. He leans against Big Al's ute, the rain plastering the hair down on his bare head, and schemes how to get the most out of the day. "Pity we didn't bring the canoes," he says, eyeing the creek, which, no longer a barely-flowing stream, is now mid-calf deep as it flows over the causeway. "Even a tyre tube would have been good," he adds, lamenting a lost opportunity for fun.

I'm finding it difficult to rekindle last night's enthusiasm, as I eye sheets of rain sweeping across the camping ground. Into the bargain, it's turned very cold. I add a couple of layers of clothing, before offering a tentative toe to the cold stream flowing under my front door.

"I was looking forward to a cooked breakfast," Roy says looking at the sorry, waterlogged barbeque in front of the tents.

A cooked breakfast was also to be a highlight for me, but fortunately, anticipating the rain, Big Al's thrown some dry wood into the back of his ute, and covered it. I make a quick sortie out into the rain and bring an armful of dry wood back under the shelter of the tarp. I sacrifice a couple of larger pieces to the water, add a few cross pieces just out of the flow, and light a small fire a few inches above the flowing stream. Then, sitting by the entrance to the tent, in a cut-down folding chair, my backside almost in the water, my feet numbed and submerged up to the ankles, but on the dry side of a curtain of precipitation flowing off Roy's big tarp, I cook bacon and eggs to the twin sizzling sounds of bacon, and hot coals falling through the bottom of the fire and into the water.

Big Al and all the others beg off riding. They've been around enough to know there's no great joy riding in heavy rain. Roy, however, is undeterred. He's always been able to balance adversity on the scales of pleasure and pain and find it coming down on the side of pleasure.

"Well, I guess we're here to ride, aren't we," he says, as if he's surveying a sun-blessed morning rather than a cold, rain-swept, miserable day. In the end, Roy, his teenage son Davy, and I are the only ones who venture out. I walk my bike across the causeway, now a foot deep in water, while Roy and Davy, shouting noisy encouragement at each other, keep their bikes upright and ride through the fast-flowing stream. We ride the flat valley floor, Roy anxious to keep me happy.

"Are you comfortable going at this pace?" he asks.

I nod and dislodge a spray of water from the peak of the baseball cap I'm wearing under my helmet. "No, this is fine," I say, furiously blinking rain out of my eyes. I'm breathing hard, but I'm far from distressed.

"Ideally you need to get your heart rate up, and keep it up," he says, shaking water off his helmet between sentences, and warming to one of his favourite subjects. "Every time you work the heart, it does it good, and the healthier it becomes. Like any other muscle, it becomes flabby and weak if you just sit around and only keep the motor turning over."

My heart is buried under layers of insulation and waterproofing, but I hope it's hearing this, and appreciating the effort I'm making on its behalf.

"Heart health is all straightforward stuff," Roy continues. "It's really just the old 'use-it-or-lose-it' principle. And anyway, isn't this just the best way to spend a day?"

My legs are numb from the cold. The rain running down the front of my neck is trying to meet up with spray from below, threatening to invade the only dry space left. Strangely, however, I'm inclined to agree with him.

We ride for a while along the flat, with hardly an undulation to be seen, then without warning, Roy turns left. At first, it's not clear where we're heading, as all that I can see in this direction is the steep valley wall rising up into misty, rain-filled clouds. I think this must be some parallel road, but suddenly the bitumen turns to dirt, and we start to climb. Just as quickly, my breathing starts to labour. Roy drops back along beside me.

"I'm going to have to get off in a minute," I say between rapid breaths, a pasty feeling settling over me like an unwelcome visitor.

To give me some respite, Roy puts a hand on my back and pushes, while I continue to merely roll the pedals around, till my breathing slowly loses its desperate edge.

"How far up does this road go?" I pant.

"A little way," Roy replies, evasively.

As soon as he stops pushing and I have to do the work myself, I feel distress return. "I'm going to have to stop," I say but with conviction this time.

"No," Roy says, equally determined. "If you get off now, you're never going to get back on. Try this," he says, and wanders sideways across the narrow dirt road. Then he makes a tight turn and wanders back across the road. "There are two ways of making it up hills you can't make it up," he says, as he resumes pushing me. "Firstly, learn to ride as slowly as you possibly can. Then, if slowness doesn't do it for you, you learn how to weave back and forth across the road, so that you flatten out the climb. Learn a combination of those two things, and you'll be able to do any hill."

He takes his hand away and that day, as the rain pours down and as we ascend at a snail's pace into the low cloud, I learn the art of riding very, very slowly up a hill. The hill seems to go on forever, but the further it heads up into the clouds, the more determined I am to stay on the bike.

"My heart needs this work," I tell myself, as I feel it pound in my chest. We climb and climb, and climb some more. I'm starting to sweat under my woollen vest, as I concentrate on the zig, the fast turn, and the slow zag across the road. I inch up, each traverse of the road gaining me a tiny increment of height, and another inch of determination. My concentration contracts to the front wheel, and seeing how slowly I can ride without falling off.

Suddenly, I sense the gradient lessen. I look up, and we're at the top amongst the clouds. Davy, who's young and fit and has ridden up and down the hill several times checking our progress, has now been patiently sitting at the top for a long while. The rain has turned sleety, and his slight frame is shivering. It is hard to believe, that in only a few short years, this skinny, shivering kid will build lean muscle onto that frame, and become the Queensland cross-country mountain bike champion many times over.

A car filled with tourists drives by and stops at a lookout. It's hard to see why they're bothering. We're above the clouds, and there's no view. They give us a what-on-earth-are-you-doing-up-here-in-the-rain look, which we return. What are any of us doing up here on a freezing rain-swept day? Well, I know I'm here because my heart needs me to be. I'm still warm from the climb, so I give my woollen vest to Davy, who is beginning to turn blue. Even Roy's eternal enthusiasm is beginning to fail, and he decides to call it a day. We turn back and retrace our steps.

Hard on the brakes, I crawl back down the hill. Because I'm no longer generating heat and my warm vest is gone, I quickly cool. By the time Big Al meets us down the bottom, I'm shivering. He has procured three hot meat pies from some unknown source in these deserted surrounds. They are close to the nicest things I have ever eaten.

He brings us one more important piece of news. "The creek's rising, everyone is leaving the camping ground."

The news gives an edge to the ride back along the valley, and we arrive in time to see the last of the four-wheel drives plough through the knee-deep water covering the causeway. Roy, of course, tries to ride across, but the force of the water pushes the bike over and sweeps him down the creek. He struggles to the far bank, the bicycle draped over one shoulder. Only one vehicle, our tents, and a trailer remain on the wrong side of the rapidly rising water. Roy doesn't seem in any particular hurry to get the car and trailer out. He wants me to resurrect the fire and boil up a brew, but he's unanimously overruled, and we begin quickly to pull down the tents. I've taken note of where the lapping water of the creek was, and when I return five minutes later, it has crept a metre further up the road.

To Roy, it's all part of the adventure, and he's in his element, enjoying things to the maximum, while all I can see is the prospect of a car, and a fully laden trailer, floating off down the creek. In the racing ever-deepening water, it's now hard to see where the edges of the causeway are. I'm given the job of struggling through the fast-flowing water to the far bank and standing on the upstream edge of the causeway. In effect, I've become a target for Roy to aim at. He enters the water at speed, heading straight at me. The tiny logical side of my brain reasons that the water will sweep the car downstream, but every other instinct wants me to leap for my life as the car arrows straight towards me. Fortunately, the water piles up against the driver's door and takes the car downstream. For a moment it seems the car and trailer are about to disappear down the creek, but it has enough forward momentum to carry it across to the far bank, where the front wheels can bite into solid ground. The back of the car and the trailer fishtail, and though one wheel of the trailer slips off the causeway, eventually everything reluctantly follows the front of the car up and out of the creek.

On the way home, Roy asks me apologetically, "I didn't put you off too much, did I?"

I'm weary, damp, and my core is still yet to heat, but a warm sense of achievement has settled upon me. I made it up a mountain, when even riding the flats would have counted as a sufficient accomplishment. Something light, essential, and long ago stolen, has been returned. I haven't been put off in the slightest, but at least I now know that riding with Roy is going to involve much more than riding a bike.

CHAPTER 2
THE LONG WAY ROUND

So far, we've touched on how we need quality heart muscle to power the pump which is our heart, and that heart muscle will stay strong if worked hard. However, that all depends on heart muscle being well supplied by healthy, good quality arteries. In this chapter, we'll discuss heart artery disease.

The heart pumps blood with its life-giving oxygen and nutrition around the body via a complex network of arteries. Muscles use this oxygen to perform work. Since the heart itself is a muscle, with its own oxygen-supplying arteries, healthy heart muscle depends on being supplied by healthy heart arteries. Every time the heart contracts, some of the blood leaves the heart and takes a quick right-angled turn to fill arteries running across the outside surface of the heart. In this way, the heart itself supplies oxygen to its own muscle.

The first thing to say about heart artery disease is that it is a process long in its development. The thing we concentrate on — a heart attack — is merely the final stage in that long progressive journey. What narrows the artery in the first place is plaque. Laid down slowly over a lifetime on the inner walls of arteries, plaque gradually narrows the vessel in the same way rust might narrow your kitchen plumbing. Eventually, if it becomes severe enough, it blocks off the artery. A heart attack is merely a diseased, narrowed, heart artery finally closing up completely. Then, when the piece of muscle supplied by that artery is deprived of blood supply, it dies. Replaced by scar tissue, it no longer contributes to the heart's contraction, and if the artery is big enough, the heart will be so compromised and shocked, that it will stop beating altogether.

Plaque is largely made up of cholesterol. Plaque and cholesterol are both words we all recognise. Cholesterol circulates in the bloodstream, with the levels in the blood partially dependent on what we eat. Whether or not plaque is deposited on the walls, and how much is deposited, depends on two main things. Firstly, the amount of cholesterol circulating. Secondly, on factors which allow circulating plaque to stick to the artery wall, either through causes related to sedentary lifestyles or processes which cause inflammation and promote 'stickiness' of the artery wall.

My professional background is in imaging hearts and blood vessels with ultrasound. Over a long career, I have looked at tens of thousands of hearts and a similar number of arteries. The trouble with artery disease, is that it does not reveal itself until it becomes relatively severe. As it slowly worsens, we remain blissfully unaware of its presence simply because we are unable to see the inside of our arteries. It is only the advent of the latest generations of imaging technology that has let us truly appreciate the internal damage that our lifestyles have inflicted on us. My background also means there are certain observations I can make, which will help you understand why and how plaque is deposited. Once armed with that knowledge, you might also be motivated to stop the slow, insidious process.

In understanding what happens to arteries, it helps to think of them as sediment-laden rivers. The analogy is a good one because, when we image inside arteries, we find plaque deposited exactly where you would find sediment deposited in a river. That is, where the flow is either slowed, or where it is disturbed, allowing slow-moving eddies to be created. The best, and most unfortunate, example of flow eddies promoting plaque deposition is in the neck. Here the big brain-supplying carotid artery divides, with one branch supplying the face while the other continuing up into the head. It is in this eddy-rich, flow-disturbed area that the plaque responsible for many of the strokes people suffer is most often deposited. As the plaque in this region slowly increases, blood flows ever faster through the narrowed area. A stroke occurs when the extremely fast-moving jet of blood knocks off bits of plaque or causes a plaque deposit to rupture. The released material plugs up smaller arteries up in the brain, with that portion of brain nourished by thc artery dying, and the functions controlled by that area of brain, lost.

The other area where the river analogy is instructive, and mirrors observation, is in the big artery in the groin supplying the leg with blood. Here, plaque is always initially deposited on the back wall of the vessel. There are two reasons why this might occur. One is that because we spend so much time asleep on our backs, gravity tends to pull the cholesterol molecules towards the back wall, where they bump along and are then more easily deposited. It may also be a result of the shape of the artery's course as it first rises up from deep in the pelvis to be close to the skin surface in the groin, then dips down again and heads deep towards the back of the thigh. Its course is shaped like a long bend in a river and, just as in a river, the sediment is deposited on the inner bank of this long curve where the blood is slower-moving.

It is important to understand that the process of plaque deposition is slow, happening molecules at a time, but is also relentless if the conditions for deposition remain. In reality, a day of inactivity is not important, nor is a week, but months and years of a lifestyle that promotes deposition of plaque do matter.

The analogy is further helpful because, just like a river, the way to stop sediment being deposited is to either regularly stir up the water by making it flow faster, or by decreasing the sediment load. This book does not touch on sediment load (the cholesterol levels in your blood), for there is a multitude of diet-related books to help you do that. It does dwell endlessly on the necessity of continually stirring up the blood so that plaque never has the opportunity to be deposited.

I ring Roy with the bad news. "I've just been on the internet, and registrations have already closed."

"That's no good," he says. "This is a ride you absolutely need to be doing."

"No, don't worry about it, I'm not too upset. Truth told, I probably would have struggled, anyway. I tend to want to lie down and rest after thirty or forty Ks. I haven't done anywhere near a hundred in one hit, before."

"Nah, you'd do a hundred — easy. It's all flat. You've been doing hills regularly, so you'll eat the flats."

"But it's all academic, anyhow. I missed the deadline for registering — simple as that."

There's a disappointed pause on the other end, and I get the impression Roy is more upset than I am. "Just come and ride, anyway."

"No, I couldn't do that," I instinctively reply. "Anyway, the first section is along the busway, and they wouldn't let you on without a number — there'll be other rides."

Half an hour later, Roy rings again. "Boyd's had a good idea," he says. "You join us after we come off the busway."

"Where does that happen?" I ask, immediately wary.

"Somewhere out in the southern suburbs," Roy says vaguely. "Anyway, Boyd's got it all sorted. It seems you just do a big loop — cross the river back up at Indooroopilly and cut across to meet us — dead easy."

Boyd, Roy, and I are old friends. We shared a house in those golden years of our early twenties, and down through the long intervening years we have all remained close. I'm entirely comfortable in their company. I already know all their idiosyncrasies. Their strengths are appreciated and enjoyed, any failings easily forgiven, allowed for and nowadays merely turned into a bottomless source of humour. As is the nature of old friendships, when the tyrannies of distance and life circumstance conspire to pause them, they merely resume again where they left off. Boyd is solid, sensible, and stable. He's the very definition of an upright, responsible citizen. Yet as if to balance an oversupply of common sense, he's an out-there adventurous spirit, who's up for almost any physical challenges. That makes him vulnerable to the kind of 'stuff' Roy enjoys. So, it's no surprise Roy has been in his ear to come riding. There is a good dynamic when the three of us get together. Singly, neither Boyd nor I can counteract Roy's excesses, but with two against one, we can nearly hold our own.

I ring up Boyd straight away.

"Well, actually," he says almost apologetically, "I think it's a doable proposition. The information on the website says we come off the busway at Eight Mile Plains, though where we head from there isn't exactly clear. But all you would need is a mobile to keep in touch, and we'd find a place somewhere to meet up. Looking at the map, if we all leave from my place, we'll all be travelling roughly the same distance to get there."

I trust Boyd. If he says something is a practical proposition, it probably is. But, strangely, the whole notion of joining the ride further down the road appeals to me on a totally different front. Never having ridden in a big group, the prospect of being in the tight confines of the busway with bikes front, back, and to each side, sounded like big trouble to someone who doesn't know the rules of riding in a pack. Me joining in later, when everyone is more spread out, might well save the organisers an unfortunate pileup on the busway.

We wake with the dawn, and Boyd's got the coffee on early. Roy's up and prowling the still-sleeping house. He's already loud and cheerful, but not yet focused on the main business at hand.

"Twenty minutes and we're out of here," Boyd greets me. Boyd's timeframes are not to be ignored, and he will be out the door by the designated time. "Helmet, gloves, and shoes?" he asks Roy.

"All sitting beside the bike," Roy answers, pleased with himself.

Boyd pushes a cup across the kitchen bench towards him.

"Tyres were on the soft side, last night," I observe.

"Yeah, I know, I'll put some more air in, in a minute," Roy replies, and Boyd pulls the coffee cup away again.

I'm looking at the map, trying to gauge relative distances, when Roy returns.

"I suppose I'd better leave about the same time as you two," I say to Roy, as he eyeballs the map from across the other side of the kitchen bench.

"We've got to ride into town and muck about getting our numbers, and then once they start, it'll take a while to get everyone into the tunnel. I'd give us a good fifteen minutes, and then head off."

I look at the map and shrug my agreement. In the end, just to be on the safe side, I only give them ten minutes.

Street maps lie — not intentionally, but by omission. Hills don't exist on their flat, pastel representations of real-world bitumen. To the unwary cyclist, not a word do they speak of the stop/go interruptions of traffic lights and stop signs, or the possibility of road works and detours. Wind does not blow across their benign surfaces. Distances, apparently equal on the page, prove far from similar in the real world. I soon realise the suburban streets I am travelling are built in hilly squares, while Roy and Boyd are moving along a busway, which arrows in a straight line through the suburbs, with carefully engineered, gentle, even gradients, all hills flattened out, all road surfaces smooth, and not a traffic light in sight.

I know I'm in trouble when their start time comes and goes and I'm still on the north side of the river, while they're already starting from the south side. There's a little map in my head, and I see them advancing steadily along the busway while I still can't seem to move my little bicycle figure from one side of the river to the other. I can only hope they're late leaving.

Foolishly relying on the flat, featureless street map, I've chosen a route which picks out every possible hill. On top of that, directions which were clear enough in my head when I consigned them to memory this morning, are becoming increasingly fuzzy.

I ride as hard as I can; hanging heavy and short, time seemingly moves faster than my legs can pump. The further south I travel, the more unfamiliar the suburbs become. I pull my way up a long hill, and breathlessly stop at the traffic lights. It takes two changes of the lights before my trembling hands have successfully punched in the right numbers on the mobile.

Boyd answers, sounding like he's out on a leisurely stroll. "Where are you?" he asks.

"Sunnybank," I pant.

"Yeah, well," he says, his voice fading as he looks around him for familiar landmarks. "I can see Mt Gravatt hill, so I reckon you must be pretty much level with us. But that means you'll have to get a wriggle on, because you're running parallel to us now, but then you're going to have to cut across east to intersect us."

All I want to do is park the bike up against the traffic light, sit for a while and recover, but somewhere up ahead are several thousand bikes already streaming off the busway, and none of them waiting for me.

Heading down unfamiliar streets, I desperately try to visualise the map I carry in my head. 'Keep heading south till you find a main road that swings off east,' seemed a straightforward enough proposition this morning, but all the roads on the left now begin to look equally main. In the end, I take an educated punt, but in no time, the road I'm following turns decidedly minor, suburban and Sunday-morning deserted, with only a few stray dog walkers, and not even a hint of the thousands of bikes I'm looking for. My hard-driving legs slow in indecision, and a decidedly lost feeling is settling over me. I start to cast an eye about the deserted streets, looking for somebody to ask directions. I'm also about to ring up Boyd to tell him I'm bushed, it's all turned too hard and they should just ride on, when suddenly, I turn a corner on the empty street. There before me is the amazing sight of a tight mass of bikes streaming straight towards me, then turning left in front of me. I've fluked it.

I ride hard towards them, find a gap in the bikes, cross over onto the footpath, and pull up breathless, and relieved. Before I even have a chance to put a foot on the ground, Boyd's unmistakable outline appears around the corner.

"Been waiting long?" he asks.

"No," I pant. "Just got here."

Roy too appears, pedalling easily. "That worked out well," he says with all the annoying certainty of someone who always expects things will work out. "Told you it would be a cinch."

"Guess what," Boyd says. "I met a friend from work, and he just wanted to see what it was like to ride on the busway. Now he's riding off home. He gave me his number, so you're even legal."

I take my time attaching the number, waiting for my breathing to settle, and feeling like I've already done my 100 Ks this morning. Then I take my legitimate place in the seemingly endless line of bikes coming round the corner and head off on my first big road ride from Brisbane, all the way to the Gold Coast.

The morning is still young and crisp, the day filled with promise and possibility. I still can't believe that, today, I'm doing a long ride like this, when only a few short months ago, one single hill was one hill too many. The lonely, desperate race through the suburbs to reach our rendezvous has now been replaced by the warm camaraderie of riding with friends, and the novel experience of joining a thousand other like-minded souls on the same cheerful expedition.

The bikes haven't yet begun to string out, and we swing our way through roundabouts like a long, solid animal of impressive size. Used to muscling bicycles out of the way, cars approaching intersections see a few bikes crossing their path and try to edge out in front, only suddenly to appreciate this large beast bearing down on them. Wisely, they pull back and wait, intimidated by the sheer size of what they're pitted against.

We're riding at my pace and Roy's content to coast beside me. "Magic, isn't it," he says.

"Perfect kind of a day," I reply.

"Sometimes, it all comes together, you know," he says in a voice that's both wistful and content. "The day turns out to be perfect, the company's perfect, and the way the legs turn the pedals feels just perfect, too. And when you get all those things happening at once, that's when you get the magic happening."

I ride along for a while, aware that Roy's watching how I'm pedalling.

"Big circles, you need to be doing much bigger circles," he says switching to his coach voice. "You're too much up on your toes, so you only push on the first part of the pedal's rotation. Do bigger, longer, circles. It'll take the strain off the inside of your thighs, and make other muscles do some of the work."

I try my best to do bigger circles, and he nods his approval.

"When we reach the next hill," he says, not yet satisfied. "I want you to start off in the gear you'd usually choose, but then drop down a couple of gears, and increase the rate you turn the pedals."

He watches me discover how much easier the climb becomes. "Last thing we'll do," he says, as if he was putting the finishing touches to a work of art, "is we'll stop at the top of the hill, I'll put your seat up a couple of centimetres, and then you should be absolutely right."

I ride on, my seat up higher, pedalling a higher cadence and doing big circles. It does feel better, and with every passing kilometre, I sense I'm making progress in this bike riding business.

"See," Roy's says, "there's more to it than just turning over the pedals, but when you get everything right, you reach this good place in your mind where pedalling the bike feels so easy, and you just want to stay on it all day."

Eventually, the continuous line of bikes begins to thin out. I start to relax and enjoy the perpetual gifts of wind and sun, and to appreciate the rhythms of riding long, flat roads. Amongst the uniform sea of Lycra around me, I also now begin to pick out the odd figure not in standard uniform, and I even identify a smattering of greybeards like me. It's encouraging to realise I'm not the only middle-aged, novice rider on the road this morning.

Despite my newfound pedalling style, I know the magic Roy was talking about is probably many more long rides away, for me. My thighs are beginning to ask tell-tale questions.

"How far do you reckon we've come?" I ask Boyd, disguising my real question of, 'how far do we still have to go?' But somehow, I know that not having reached halfway, I shouldn't be making 'are we there yet?' enquiries.

"Halfway stop should be coming up very soon," Boyd confirms, to the relief of my legs.

I linger over my legitimately-acquired bun and walk out some of the leg stiffness, and once fuelled and watered, I start to feel reinvigorated. After a few stretches to remove the knots in my back and shoulders, I throw my leg back over the seat and head off with renewed enthusiasm.

"Car drivers," Roy suddenly says, thinking out loud.

I look across at him. He's shaking his head, sadly. "None of them gets away with it, you know."

"Get away with what?" I ask, readying myself for a conversation about driver behaviour.

"Plaque," he replies as if the answer should be obvious to me. "They're driving around laying it down, while we're out here stripping it off."

"Right," I say, unsure quite how to contribute.

"See, they'll be out in the car this morning — off down to the shop to get the papers and a bottle of milk. Then, later on, they'll take grandma out for a Sunday drive. Tonight, they'll drop down in the car and pick up some takeaway for dinner, and in-between times they'll be sitting on the couch, never getting the heart rate up, and slowly laying the plaque down. But what they don't ever realise is none of them gets away with it — not a single one of them."

I can hear a combination of passion and sorrow in his voice, and he seems genuinely upset. "Yeah, it's true; they're not doing themselves any favours. It's such an insidious process," I say, while I feel my own heart pounding away in my chest for all its worth.

"That's the point," he agrees. "It happens slowly, but it's also relentless."

We've started to accelerate down a hill. Roy's holding on with one hand, his body half turned towards me and gesticulating at me with the other, just as if we were side by side on a couch, instead of moving along at sixty kilometres an hour. More disconcertingly, with the noise of the wind whistling past our helmets, he's moved alarmingly close to me so I can hear.

"That's why we've got to keep stirring it up."

I steal a quick sideways glance and think about attempting a nod, but wisely, I wait till we bottom out, and I can safely look across and agree. "Trouble is, people are unaware they're slowly killing themselves," I say, as I relax the iron-tight grip I've had on the handlebars.

"Exactly," he says. "See, people have got absolutely the wrong idea about it all." He's becoming more expressive now we're on the flat, and he's sitting up, both hands off the handlebars to aid making the point. "They think heart disease is something they catch if they're unlucky, but the truth is, nobody gets away with anything — there's a payback for everything …" He stands up on the pedals for a few quick strokes to better enjoy leaning into the long sweep of a roundabout and then lets me catch up again before he finishes the sentence, "… and everyone." Roy's a nurse and a deeply compassionate and caring person. Like me, he too has a professional interest in these things.

"See, never be fooled by how pink and healthy people look on the outside. If they carry a heavy sediment load because they eat cholesterol-rich foods and they don't stir it up regularly, then they just don't get away with it. Simple as that."

He's preaching to the converted, and the conversation is making me feel good about being out here 'doing stuff'.

"So there they are, out in their cars and by the end of the day, a few more molecules of cholesterol have been deposited, while we're all out here, stripping it back off, and having so much fun doing it."

I start to look differently at the cars driving past. I've picked up a little of Roy's sorrow, and begin to feel pity for all those poor people, driving everywhere and slowly but relentlessly depositing plaque on the walls of their arteries.

I'm still enjoying the glad-hearted magic of the day, but somewhere halfway through the second fifty Ks, my legs begin to send out the first signals of distress, and my thighs set up a plaintive whine at the prospect of each hill that no big-circled, high cadence approach will fix. For a while now, a distinct sense of discomfort has become apparent where my bottom meets the bike seat, and I find myself up and off the saddle at even the hint of a hill. But, as with all achievement, the more effort involved and the greater the pain in reaching the goal, the greater the sense of triumph. I wouldn't mind if the finish were around the corner, but the tall towers of the Gold Coast are not yet in sight. So I set myself merely to make it up the next hill. The transition from extreme enjoyment to moderate struggle happens rapidly. *Are we there yet* becomes a preoccupation.

"Don't keep looking up," Boyd says, sensing I'm beginning to struggle. "Just keep the pedals turning over, and eventually you'll get there."

The second fifty is so much longer than the first, but eventually open fields give way to suburban streets, the tall towers come into sight and soon we've even moved under their shadows. The final kilometres stretch out in agonising slowness. But finally, Roy's saying, "C'mon we're all going to sprint the last few hundred yards," and in a fast and furious finale of speed and emotion, we cross the finish line.

It's hard for me to believe that, this morning, I was in Brisbane and now I've pedalled all the way to the Gold Coast. I dismount the bike, my legs jellied and not part of me.

"Told you, you'd do it easy," Roy says, looking maddeningly fresh, hardly sweating.

I sit on the grass, afraid of what might happen if I try to stand up again. Boyd appears with a lifesaving cup of coffee. He's looking midway between the pristine glow of Roy and my spent prostration; enough energy to be still on his feet but with the redness of effort on each patch of exposed skin. Strangely, I've given no thought to what happens next. All I know is we're having lunch at Roy's, and then travelling home by train.

"What do you think?" Roy says. "I could ring up Heather to come and pick us up, or we could just all ride home to my place and have a late lunch."

The question is loaded, and I wait for Boyd to voice dissent, but he doesn't.

"It's not far, only twenty Ks. I do it all the time," Roy says cheerily. "You'll do it easy." He mistakes the look I'm giving him. "No, finish the coffee — no hurry."

Boyd helps me to my feet and I stand, feet apart to cope with the swaying.

"I suppose the more stripping I do, today, the better," I say, resigned.

"Stripping what?" Boyd asks.

"Plaque," Roy and I reply simultaneously.

CHAPTER 3
DIRT DISEASE

BEFORE WE CONTINUE EXPLORING THE NITTY-GRITTY OF HEART health, let's examine for a moment the other question posed by this book: Why cannot old age be an active time of life, and why do we instinctively believe we can no longer involve ourselves in high-grade physical activity as we grow old? Why can't that work-free, raising-children-free, time-rich part of our lives mark a return to the carefree, freewheeling days of our youth? Is the wind in the hair enjoyment of a fast descent on a bicycle somehow any less exciting when you're old? Is not our enjoyment of the great outdoors enhanced with age, not reduced, and doesn't the ability to still be able to participate in physical activity make that activity even more enjoyable?

I have a teenage memory of watching my father play soccer on a beach. I think it is a memory which has stuck, simply because it was accompanied by the thought that this was something very unusual for a man in his fifties. That I should have had that thought is reflective of a view of old age that still lingers with us; it still is the dominant view of aging. That is, that old age is a time to slow down, retreat to the couch and take things easy. So we do, and as we follow that path, not surprisingly, bodies shrink, shoulders become more rounded and stooped, bones become brittle, and people start to appear old and fragile.

We carry both the thought and attitudinal legacy with us — old people are delicate and inhabit increasingly fragile bodies. Hearts are worn out by age and should never be strained. But with all chicken and egg stories, it is a matter of what came first. This is not to deny that bodies age, but it is to deny the easy corollary — that high-grade physical activity can no longer be undertaken by aging bodies. In fact, as you will see in the coming chapters, our bodies have a tremendous capacity to adapt to the demands we place on them. In terms of heart health, our hearts will not wear out if we work them; they will, in fact, thrive with ongoing and increased physical activity.

There's another thing that sticks in the memory. My parents' conversations about their sedentary friends were peppered with talk of strokes and heart attacks. I also remember the way this was discussed, as if these events were no more than bad luck, akin to receiving a random losing ticket in the lottery of life. Like catching a cold or being hit by lightning, it was something that could happen to anyone. However, as we continue to come to grips with the mechanisms of heart disease, we'll find nothing could be further from the truth: lifestyle and outcomes are inexorably linked, and heart disease is both entirely predictable and mostly preventable. We don't escape the way we live, and we bear the rewards and costs of how we live as we move into the back end of our lives.

The importance of understanding this intimate and inevitable link between lifestyle and outcomes can't be overstated. We tend to only think of retirement planning in financial terms yet, compared with the importance of planning for health and quality of life as we age, financial security pales into relative insignificance. We need to start the work of quality-of-life retirement planning early, for if we pay attention to heart health as we move into middle age, we reap the rewards of quality of life and longevity in old age.

My dad remained healthy and vigorous well into his nineties. He lived till ninety-six, and it was not his heart that killed him.

Roy's sitting in the passenger seat of the car, half-turned so as to include me in the conversation. "How're you feeling?" he asks.

"I'm good," I reply. In fact, all I'm feeling is an honest, pleasant weariness instead of my usual post-ride shattered state, but for some reason, Roy has called a halt early, before exhaustion replaced enjoyment as the day's dominant sensation.

"You know, I reckon I probably rode sixty hilly Ks today," I say, though in my own mind I'm taking off some of that distance to compensate for Roy having pushed me up any steep hills.

"You would have done at least that," Roy agrees. "You're doing real good for someone just getting their riding legs."

"You know what," I muse. "I think I need to get just that little bit fitter, so that when I ride up a decent hill I don't have the feeling at the top that I absolutely have to stop and catch my breath. If I could just get fit enough to get up and over the hills without stopping at the top, I'd be happy."

"No!" Roy exclaims with unexpected passion, and turns further around in his seat towards me, his face suddenly intense. "That's not where we're aiming. None of us are stopping where we are now, or even where we'd like to be. We all have to keep going and ramp it steadily up so that each year between now and when we turn sixty, we're fitter than we were the year before. That's where we all should be aiming." He turns back towards Boyd, looking for support.

Boyd's opinions are usually worth hearing. Measured and thoughtful, Boyd tends to quickly skewer woolly thinking of any description. "I don't think there's any physiological reason why we can't," Boyd says, in measured agreement. "In fact, just the other day I was reading about a runner who used to keep a detailed record of his performances over a large number of years, and he claimed his times didn't significantly decline till he was into his seventies."

"See," Roy crows. "That's the thing — there's absolutely no reason why we can't be fitter at sixty than we were at fifty." An evangelical light has appeared in his eyes, and he's rapidly winding up to a hot crescendo of enthusiasm. "Into our sixties and even till we're pushing seventy, we can be out there doing stuff, getting ourselves fitter and fitter." His hand hits the car roof, as he makes clear to Boyd and me just how high our fitness level could go. Then he turns back around towards me, looking for a response.

"Well, I'm all in favour of getting fit," I say, smart enough to know that agreement with a proposition posited nearly ten years in the future will cost me nothing. With the insincerity of a politician who believes he will never be held to account for glib promises, I blunder on. "It would be absolutely great to get really, really fit."

I can see Roy's eyes grow even brighter at the prospect that we're all on the same page. "There's this book I'm reading, about this ultra-marathon runner," he says with a mixture of awe and enthusiasm.

But my guilty eyes have dropped, and I'm suddenly feeling the weight and tiredness of my years. I wisely sink deep into the back seat and let the true believers in the front launch into an animated conversation about the merits of extreme exercise.

"Turn left here, Boyd," Roy suddenly says. "I want to show you the mountain bike track at Kooralbyn where we race. It's just a little detour, and we've got time."

Kooralbyn will eventually become a shrine of good memories for all three of us. But as Roy stands on a small bridge near the start/finish line, sniffing the air of memory, and for all the world looking as if he's recalling something particularly exquisite, all Boyd and I can appreciate are a few low, drab hills. Eventually, Roy lets us in on his reverie.

"I remember when I first started racing. I had this old bike — no suspension, nothing. Everything was wrong about the bike, and everything was wrong about me, too. I had absolutely no idea. I just used to throw the leg over and go for it as hard as I could. So the very first race, I came flying down this hill, here, chasing someone for all I was worth. I followed them way too fast into the corner, and I lost it. Like it might have been the tenth time the same thing had happened that day. That was just how much clue I didn't have, but this time when I picked the bike up, instead of hopping back on and heading out for another lap, I just walked it over here under the trees, sat down, and didn't get up again. I had trashed myself that badly, and got way too overheated and dry. My heart was going a thousand beats a minute and wouldn't slow. I probably sat there for a full half an hour drinking and pouring water over myself, before I could even think of getting up. That was such a great day, eh?"

He returns to the present, his hand motioning across to the hill on our left. "You don't get much idea from here, but the track works its way back and forward across the hill, and then heads up over the top and out the back. We'll go for a ride, and that'll give you a better idea," he adds, as if this idea has only just occurred.

Boyd and I, weary from the day's ride, are looking less than enthusiastic, but Roy's already halfway over to the car to unload the bikes.

"Let's go do a lap — you'll love it, I promise."

We head out on a dusty track that leads us up and over the nearest low hill. Luckily, my good-for-all-purposes machine has tyres with some thickness, and Boyd and I are soon blowing hard as we follow Roy over the top and onto a long winding downhill run. As I negotiate the tight corners, barely under control, I'm soon aware that riding these loose, dusty slopes, with their rollercoaster thrills, carries with it a faint but pure imprint of things that once made me smile. It is as if the elemental interaction of dirt, speed, and fresh air, is stirring memories direct from the highlights tape of life, and I like the feeling.

Roy stops at the bottom of the downhill run, leans on the front of the bike, and readies himself for some hard sell. "See, you both came down that slope easy as anything. I tell you what, handling bikes is stuff we instinctively all know how to do. Nothing much more to learn really, just a bit of finessing of what's already there." He glances over at us, looking for agreement, but I'm still stuck back at the 'easy as anything' part. "I reckon this is one of the best things of not being part of the computer generation," he continues, a wistful look entering his eye as he recalls the sunshine days of our youth. "We were just so lucky, weren't we, that we belonged to the generation of children who never came home until it got dark."

As is often the case with Roy, enlightenment comes to him even as he speaks, and we soon become beneficiaries of the real-time apprehension of yet another of life's truths being nailed down and filed away.

"It is true, isn't it?" he says, struck by the import of the revelation. "Everything in life has to have a payback, and now, even with all those years in between, we get to do this kind of stuff, because of the things we did way back then."

I'm still breathing hard from the climb before the downhill run, and my head is still down, but I manage to glance over at Boyd. I immediately recognise another fifteen-year-old enjoying one of life's delayed paybacks. Although I know Roy is much too quick to ascribe skills to me that I don't possess, I suspect I'll be replaying that sweeping downhill run as a pleasant way to drift off to sleep tonight.

"The big difference between then and now is that I wasn't a hundred kilos when I was young," Boyd jokes, but I can hear the breathless enjoyment in his voice.

Roy, though, hasn't worked out that he has already won, and resumes the sell. "No, seriously, there's nothing major to learn. It's just a matter of finessing what's already there, and you'd both be riding a track like this with the best of them."

"It was good fun," I confess for both of us. "But we'd need to be a whole lot fitter to really enjoy it."

Roy is quiet for a second, momentarily thrown by the unexpected positive response. "There's a six-hour event coming up next month," he says quietly, his voice pitched low to minimize any threat. "You can enter three-man teams. Each person does a lap and then hands over to the next rider. It's great fun, but, like you say, you'll both need to put in some effort between now and then."

It takes a few seconds before I comprehend the three-man team he had in mind is Boyd, me, and him. "We'd be a danger to everyone else, never mind ourselves," I respond with reflex alarm.

"Not an issue," Roy replies, dismissively. "But, listen, if we're serious about being fitter at sixty than we are at fifty, then this is something we all absolutely need to do."

Boyd is silent, but a quiet smile is threatening.

"Well, I suppose if it's something we absolutely need to be doing …" I say.

Down my short, steep driveway, hard left into the garage, miss the corner of the washing machine, hard right turn, squeeze through the side garage door, quickly adjust direction to miss the big pot plant at the base of the stairs, shoot out into the yard and circle back around our big concrete water tank. At least that was the theory. The reality was fast down the hill, hard left into the garage, suddenly realise how narrow was the doorway, panic, hit the brakes, try to chicken out at the last moment, fail even to do that, lift the forearm to protect the head, hit something hard and unyielding. But as with all these things, endless repetition seemed to be the key. By trial and error, I found that too slow was just as disastrous as too fast. Too slow, and the wobbling exit through the side door would see my shoulder or the handlebars hung up on the doorpost. Too fast, if I was lucky I'd make it through the narrow doorway, but the front wheel would fail to negotiate the rock-like pot plant at the foot of the stairs. The bruises on my shoulders were soon developing bruises of their own, but just occasionally I'd get the speed and the steering right, and it felt so good as I weaved and shimmied my way out into the yard. At least I now knew that if on the track, I came across any misplaced washing machines or encountered narrow doorways, I'd handle them with ease.

As the day of the event nears, I find there are certain aspects of mountain biking which aren't letting me sleep too well, and I need them clarified. "I'm trying to envisage how to land if I end up over the handlebars," I say to Roy. "I mean, do you try to flick yourself over like in a summersault, and land on your feet, or is it simply a matter of just getting the hands out in front and making sure you don't land on your head?"

"Usually everything happens too quick," Roy says, and the way he screws his eyes up, it's as if he's never had the question put to him before. "One second it's all good, then it all goes bad, and you're over the front of the bike."

"Yes, but," I say, none the wiser, "what usually happens with the landing?"

"What happened when you were a kid?" Roy asks. "You must have had busters then."

"Lots, I suppose," I reply. "But I just don't remember what happens."

"Did you ever used to hurt yourself?"

"Never seriously."

"Well, there you are — you're all prepared. You learned all you need to know, then. It might all happen quick, but you'll find survival instinct kicks right in. You'll grab some bushy little tree to break your fall, or fling yourself onto the only soft patch in the middle of a whole bunch of rocks, and you'll wonder, how did I manage to pull that off without getting hurt? The truth is you've already learned all you need to know, and you knew it by the time you were ten."

I'm half-convinced, but my brittle bones know they don't want to test that truth.

Boyd and I set up camp on the edge of the little tent city that's sprung up near the start. Feeling faintly lost and looking for the registration area, we walk around in a milling mass of bikes and young fit muscular riders. We're also feeling decidedly out of place, but trying hard to act as if we're not the interlopers we feel we are. Like walking into a black-tie event dressed in jeans and tee-shirt, we're waiting for someone to say, 'What are you old people doing here, with those unsuitable bikes, and dressed that way?' Yet nobody seems to be looking sideways at us, and the whole place has such a good, joyful, fun vibe that we soon relax.

We manage to register ourselves, and by trial and error, work out how to attach the backing plates to the bikes, and where to stick the Velcro so that the number we'll exchange after each lap will stay attached. Boyd is looking at his watch, beginning to show concern that Roy and Davy haven't shown up, and soon I hear him on the mobile.

"You do realise that the registration desk closes in ten minutes, and the race starts in forty," I hear him say, then the frown which has appeared on his forehead, suddenly deepens. "But that's probably nearly thirty minutes away," he groans into the phone, with a mixture of annoyance and concern.

"Where is he?" I ask.

"He's still the other side of Beaudesert," Boyd replies in disbelief.

"Well, that means you'll have to be first up then," I quickly announce, trying to sound as if that was the obvious fall-back position. "So you'd better head down, now, to the rider's briefing."

Roy finally arrives, and immediately launches into a full round of back-slapping greetings, before Boyd stops him short, and points him towards the registration area. Young Davy has already put his bike together quickly and gone off to find his team, but for Roy the ritual heartfelt greeting of friends takes precedence over a minor issue such as missing the start. Eventually, though, the sight of all the riders beginning to gather down near the start turns his attention to the mechanics of getting ready, and he starts to ferret in the back of the car, managing to turn out shoes and gloves and a helmet. He has a bad moment until he locates his front wheel hiding under a blanket. Then, even as the lead riders form themselves up, he heads off to sweet-talk the ladies at the registration desk and recover the situation. As will become our repeating lot in life, Boyd and I do all the other things that will get him to the starting line in time, and as the starter begins the final countdown, Roy appears from between the tents, we slap his number on the front of the bike, and hand him his helmet and gloves. As the gun fires, he ducks into the mass of riders somewhere near the front, and he's off.

The solid clump of riders elongate up the hillside as they head up and over the top. As the riders disappear, we turn with the other spectators to leisurely stroll back towards our tent, but the pace quickens as Boyd realizes that in half an hour, he will be heading out up the same hill, and so he'd better ready himself.

"I've come to the view that an hour's practice isn't quite enough preparation for what's going to happen out there," Boyd says, with resigned gallows humour.

"And I bet he didn't take us on any of the hard technical bits when we went for that ride," I add, a queasy fear of the unknown beginning to tighten into apprehension.

"I just hope I don't knock anyone else off their bike," Boyd says, articulating a fear we both have.

"Roy says people will work out very quickly we need to be given a wide berth," I offer encouragingly.

Powered by nervous energy, Boyd begins to pace around the tent.

"Plenty of time," I say as we both begin searching the empty hill for returning riders. But, as it happens, there isn't plenty of time. Much sooner than we expect, the gun riders are pouring back down the hill, young Davy amongst them. Right on their tails, Roy roars back in and slides broadside in front of Boyd, grinning.

I hardly have time to say, "Good luck," and Boyd's off up the hill, to meet whatever fate awaits.

Back at the tent, Roy throws the bike on the grass and in one continuous movement, looking for something cool and wet, he opens an esky. He's in his element. "Isn't it great — the old guys out there, kicking the young guys' butts."

"You had a good time, then?" I ask.

"First round's always slow with all that traffic," he answers, then laughs, and the way he laughs tells me there is a good story about to spill out. "See, there was this young guy," he begins, but interrupts himself and quickly downs a mouthful of apple juice. "We're out the back, about halfway round, and everyone's beginning to string out. I'm behind someone who's obviously gone out way too fast, and now he's suffering." He manages to pull off one shoe and one glove, but he seems to want to be on the move while telling the story, so he walks around with one shoe still on. "So, I'm waiting for a place to slip past, when suddenly some smart idiot decides he'll jump up on the bank and try to take us both at the same time. I can see it's never going to happen for him. He's suddenly got this tree right there, right, but he wants to get past so bad that, instead of just falling in behind us again, he tries to drop back down onto the track. Only he's going to drop down right on top of both of us and take us out. So, I end up doing all this heroic stuff so he can drop in between us, and it all ends up good." He removes the other shoe and throws it over towards the bike.

So that they stay together, I quietly throw its partner across to join it.

"But I'm not going to let him away with it, right. So as soon as we're both past the other guy, I'm off chasing him as hard as I can." Roy manages several mouthfuls of juice before he continues the story. "I finally catch him on the long hill right out the back." He looks at me to see that I get where he means, and then he remembers that I haven't been out on the course, yet. "So, anyway, I'm letting him know I'm there, right up close behind, chasing him up the hill. I wait till we're about three-quarters of the way up, then I get up on the pedals, and I take him. I'm still going hard when I suddenly realise I'm dying, but I've still got this hill happening, and what's more I've reached the bit right at the top where it jags up suddenly. But I'm not about to let him know I'm bonking big time, so I stay up on the pedals, even though there's nothing left in the legs, and I just manage to get the bike up onto the flat before I die completely."

"And did he come back at you?"

"Nah, never saw him again."

I quiz him about the dangers that I might encounter out there, but with a shake of the head, he assures me there's nothing worth mentioning.

"Sure there's nothing too technical?" I ask.

"No, it's all good — you're going to have so much fun."

I move down to the start long before Boyd is due in. There's a steady stream of riders returning down the hill, and just as I'm wondering whether he's met with disaster, he appears. There's dust all down one side, but nothing red is seeping through. He wearily slaps our number onto my backing plate. "Enjoy," he says as if he's only enough energy left for a single word, and so I set off with a strange mixture of terror and exhilaration turning over the pedals for me.

"Nice and slow," I remind myself, as I ease my way up the first hill. It's a wide track with room for anyone to pass, and I'm moving just fast enough to stop the front wheel from wobbling. I stay disciplined until I reach the narrow single track where passing is harder, and the pressure of people coming up behind begins to speed me up more than I can cope with. Along with knocking people off, holding everyone up is my other big concern, but somehow people manage to steer a way around me with minimum disruption. Without exception, everyone is totally polite as they squeeze past. However, pushing hard trying to stay out of everyone's way sends me into the red zone, and soon I have to stop. I have a drink, polish the sunnies and, with the benefit of the training I've been doing, the breathing settles right down again, and off I go once more.

I grip the handlebars hard on the downhills, bounce my way over the rocky technical sections and, to my amazement, the bike and I stay together. Each little triumph adds to the realization that perhaps I can actually do this. Clumsy and uncertain, I negotiate the tight corners with tight jerky trepidation, but as the kilometres pass, gradually my iron grip starts to relax. I'm walking all the steeper hills, feeling slightly embarrassed that everyone else stays on the bike as they move effortlessly past me. But on the long, shallow, winding downhill slopes, a growing confidence lets the brakes go, the bike starts to run free, and I begin increasingly to enjoy myself.

I return in one piece, and Boyd and I exchange stories of the experience. Boyd has a few more dust patches than I, and claims a spectacular face plant after catching a pedal on a tree. All I've got to show is a chunk missing from my shin when a foot slipped from the pedal, but otherwise, all I have to boast about are a few low-speed offs.

Roy comes in from his second round a bit more subdued.

I comment on it.

"There's a big log," he says meaningfully.

I know which one he means. "You can ride around it, if you want," I say.

"Yeah, but," he replies, and shrugs, "usually I land it pretty good. It was just the front wheel twisted on me when I came down, and from that point it was all over."

"What did you hurt?" I ask.

"Winded more than anything," he replies, then burps loudly to signify he's now fully recovered. Roy asks me about the dust patch on my shoulder.

"There's a steep little drop down into a gully," I explain, "then the track turns sharply back on itself. But I was so intent on negotiating the drop, that I went right through the turn."

"See," Roy says knowingly, "watching what comes next is important. Even before you dropped down, your eyes should have moved on to take in what you have to deal with next."

I file away that information, and next time back I'm able to say, "Got the drop-off right, got the turn right, but I came out of it much too fast and my front wheel ended up on the wrong side of a big rock, which threw me across into a bushy tree." By the third lap, I can claim I held the drop together, made the turn, kept up a good speed, slipped inside the rock but found I was in much too high a gear to make it up the far bank, and I ended up hugging a tree to stop from rolling back down. However, on my last lap, everything comes together; I drop down, steer smoothly through the corner, miss the rock, hit the far slope of the gully in just the right gear and explode up and over the top. And how good did it all feel!

By the second round, I've even worked out my strategy for getting around the course. Ride the flats much more slowly than feels right. Keep enough of my meagre supply of puff in reserve for the hills, so I don't have the embarrassment of walking them, and simply enjoy to the maximum anything that points downhill. On the third round, as I ease my way into a tight downhill corner, someone cuts inside me at speed in a way that doesn't seem possible on such a tight curve.

"How ya goin'?" young Davy asks as he speeds by. Fortunately, the track's pointing gently downhill and is straight, so I chase after him at an unsustainable speed, asking him if that's as fast as he can go and loudly threatening to pass him at any time. We're catching a female rider rapidly, and I see her shoulders tense as the yelling, squealing train arrives on top of her. Davy simply hops up on the bank without slowing, and I, in noisy pursuit, recklessly follow. Eventually, the track turns up again, and I have to abandon the chase. I stop for a minute, let the breathing settle, then once more throw my leg over the bike. I'm having absolutely the best of times.

A survivor's euphoria follows me around the last lap. The course has lost any sense of terror, I'm beginning more and more to let the brakes go, and I feel my tight grip on the handlebars is also relaxing. Roy was right; instinctively, I do know how to do this, and it is fun as promised. As I put the foot down to try and give Roy one more lap before the six hours are up, I know two things. One is that I'm going to do more of this. The other is I'm going to get a whole lot fitter before I do.

CHAPTER 4
BAKED BEANS AND BATTERIES

SO BACK TO HEARTS, AND TIME TO TALK ABOUT HOW THE PUMP works, and why unhealthy heart muscle is such a bad thing for good pump operation. In a future chapter we'll talk about the way resistance in the downstream arterial pipes changes pump pressures, causing what is commonly termed high blood pressure, but here we'll examine the role of heart muscle quality in changing some of the other internal pump pressures. This is a little technical, but concentrate just for a page or two, and you'll grasp why heart muscle needs to stay healthy.

The heart has four chambers. Of these, two are large and are the pumping chambers of the heart, the ventricles. One of these, the left, is thick-walled and very muscular. It needs to be this way because this chamber sends the blood on its journey to the far extremities of the body. Typically, when this chamber contracts, it exerts a force of 120 to 140 millimetres of mercury (mmHg.). This is what is known as systolic blood pressure. The other main pumping chamber, the right ventricle, only has to push blood through the lungs and return it to the other side of the heart. It, therefore, is less thick-walled, and less strong. When it contracts, it exerts a lower internal pressure of 20 to 30 mmHg. The other two chambers, the atria, are not involved in pumping blood. They are merely tasked with collecting the returning blood from the body or lungs and pushing it through a valve into one or other pumping chamber. These smaller chambers are thin-walled, non-muscular and operate with a very low pressure of only 3 to 5 mmHg. The following sentence is the main thing to grasp in understanding why healthy heart muscle becomes increasingly more important as we age, and unhealthy muscle more problematic. The heart is a pump which generates internal pressures within its chambers, and an intimate relationship exists between the quality of the heart muscle and these pressures.

So let's see how that relationship affects how the heart functions. When heart muscle contracts, the two big pumping chambers, the ventricles, simultaneously send blood on a journey — right side to the lungs and back, left around the entire body. They then refill in two stages. First, the muscle of the ventricles actively relaxes, springs back, and sucks blood in from the smaller chambers, the atria. Then the atria give a little squeeze and complete the filling of the ventricles just before the ventricles contract again. When we are young, the ventricles largely fill from the suck of the muscle relaxing, and are only topped up from the small squeeze of the atria.

As a natural process, as hearts age, the heart muscle becomes less springy, sucks less well, and the atria have to push harder, doing more of the work to completely fill the ventricles. The heart functions best within a narrow range of pressures, but hearts generally cope well with the ageing process. The internal pressures do not alter much as long as the heart muscle stays healthy.

While we might get away with things when we're young, there's an increasing price to be paid if we don't pay attention to heart muscle health as we age. The processes involved are gradual and slow, but are insidious. If we add a lifestyle of inactivity to natural aging, the body will deliver to you the heart muscle appropriate to that lifestyle. Never having to work hard, it becomes a much less toned piece of muscle than it would be if you were working it well. It becomes stiffer, and does not relax as well. Theoretically, you might think this doesn't really matter as, because you are now sedentary, you don't need a strongly-muscled pump. However, muscle that loses tone, power, and springiness, becomes stiffer and loses some of the suck capacity that it once had. This changes the internal pressures. More and more of the work of filling the pumping chambers falls to the contraction of the two smaller chambers. To adequately do this task, the pressures in these smaller chambers rise — rises that are not without consequence. In these thin-walled, non-muscular chambers, the increased filling pressures cause a very slow enlargement of the atria.

When the two atria enlarge, this in turn, has consequences for the heart's electrics. The electrical impulses causing the heart to beat are generated in the atria and run around the atrial walls. Stretching of the walls as the chambers enlarge can alter and interfere with these electrical pathways. Up to this point, there are often no symptoms; often the first indication that someone has anything amiss with their hearts is that they develop rhythm abnormalities, most notably atrial fibrillation which is the losing of the small chambers' contraction altogether.

The good news is that this need not be the end of the story. Much of this is reversible, due to this being a dynamic process caused by changing pressures, which in turn is often driven by muscle health. Returning the heart muscle to health by working it harder will aid it in the task of sucking properly, and a heart chamber that sucks better will reduce the pressure needed to fill it. Hence, regularly working the heart harder can halt and even reverse the enlargement of the atria.

We spend a lot of hospital resources in treating hearts which progress beyond this point. If deterioration is not reversed in the early stages, feedback mechanisms operate, whereby rhythm abnormalities further increase the pressures in the atria, which further enlarge the chambers in a vicious tit-for-tat process that permanently locks in the abnormal rhythm. Such hearts can continue to limp along for years, but they are prone to have clots form in their poorly-functioning enlarged corners, which can then break away and shoot up into the brain. This mechanism, along with the previously discussed problem of plaque breaking free from the neck arteries, are the two main causes of stroke. This outcome is very, very common. The cardiac wards in our hospitals are filled with such hearts, and the costs, in terms of disability and death, are huge.

However, if treated well, stiff muscle can become more compliant, and the process reversed. Frequent, consistent, moderate exercise, of the kind which results in us breathing hard, signals to the heart how it now needs to perform, and will often be sufficient to do the job. There are guidelines available that suggest as little as twenty to thirty minutes of moderate exercise each day is enough. As we will examine later, when we look at what downstream resistance to blood flow does to the pressures in the two pumping chambers, exercise will also improve the state of the whole vascular tree, and reduce resistance to blood flow, which has good consequences for systolic blood pressure, and a properly functioning heart.

Going right over the top with exercise will probably yield little in the way of extra benefit for heart health, but is a spirit lifter and a soul refresher. It therefore is recommended for no other reason other than just because it can be so much fun.

Boyd and I sit on the cafe verandah, drinking coffee and into our second round of scones and cream. In anticipation of a big afternoon ahead, we're spooning the cream on thickly, with guiltless enjoyment. However, alongside the pleasant anticipation of a ride and the pleasures of fuelling up, there's a troubled edge of anxiety stalking our upbeat mood.

"How big are these climbs?" Boyd asks.

"From memory, the lookout sits at about twelve hundred metres," I reply.

Boyd pauses the coffee cup short of his mouth. "And it's straight up?" he asks. "Zero to twelve hundred in one hit?"

"Two climbs," I expand, "with a short section of flat between them. But each of the climbs is about as bad as it gets — straight up with no respite. Just steep and nasty and mean." I employ all the head shaking adjectives I can think of, because I want to leave him in no doubt about the challenge ahead.

"And you've ridden up these hills?" he asks with barely concealed scepticism.

"No," I erupt, laughing. "I had a go at the first climb, but piked less than half way up. After that, I was support car material all the way."

Boyd nods, and for a moment turns quiet. We're both very aware there will be no support car today.

"Could be a long walk up that hill," I muse, with an anxious sigh.

"But you've been putting in plenty of time on the bike, lately," Boyd says, intending encouragement. But I find his raised eyebrows also asking just how weak the weakest link thinks he'll be, today.

"Yes, I'm in so much better a state now," I insist. It's a nervous confidence I'm expressing, though. For I might well have come a long way in a short time, but this afternoon is going to test out my legs and lungs in a way that even an all-day ride on the flat couldn't. "What does he want to do this particular ride for, anyway?" I ask, my unease breaking through into mild annoyance.

"I don't know," Boyd replies. "From what he said to me, I think someone told him there were big hills involved, and for some reason, that's why it appeals. I think he's simply keen for us to be doing hills."

"Well, he's got his wish today," I confirm.

Boyd looks at his watch, and then across to the car park opposite, where the rendezvous has been arranged. "How long do you think the ride will take?" he asks.

"From memory, we stopped here, at Boonah, before lunch, and we just made it in to Queen Mary Falls by dark."

Boyd looks again at his watch. "Well I haven't got any lights on the bike," he says.

"Me neither, but we'll still be on track as long as we get away soon," I say with more conviction than I feel.

The designated meeting time of twelve is quickly receding. It's now getting on for one o'clock, and Roy's still a no-show. Neither of us is too upset. This isn't the usual Roy lateness. Today, he's coming off a nightshift, and the plan was always for him to grab a few hours sleep, and then we'd meet. However, not starting till lunchtime always meant we'd be cutting it fine at the back end of the day. There's a stiff, cold westerly blowing straight into our faces, and the mid-winter sun will fall away quickly once we're in the shadow of the mountains. Add to that, the likelihood that I'll blow up on the climbs, means there are some very good reasons why anxiety should be stalking my upbeat mood.

The scones are so good that we're even thinking of yet one more round, when Roy roars into the car park. By the time we've sauntered over for the usual laughing high five, back-slapping round of greetings, he's disgorged across the surface of the car park, a pile of wheels, bike frames and sundry other bits and pieces to be assembled into two working mountain bikes, for him and Davy.

"Sorry, got busy doing stuff," he says, handing me a carrier that he indicates he wants fixed to the back of one of the bikes.

"Get any sleep?" I ask.

"Nah," he replies, as if sleep was an unwelcome intrusion into having fun. "Sleep all the better tonight."

One tyre is flat, and he unsuccessfully turns out various boxes looking for a spare tube. I've put relatively skinny tyres on my all-purpose bike, and can't help, so Boyd reluctantly hands over his only spare tube. Roy pumps away merrily, his attention on telling stories and filling us in on what's been happening, when bang! The tube goes off like a rifle shot. Roy falls about laughing and tells me how far I jumped. That leads into a few other stories about tubes going off in various circumstances, then when he's sucked every ounce of humour from the situation he turns his attention to the sorry problem that lies flat before him. He dispatches Davy to look around town for a bike shop.

"What do you need a carrier for, anyway?" I ask as my four thumbs struggle with the contraption he's given me to attach to his bike.

"Well, I don't want to carry everything on my back," he replies.

"You do know that there's a restaurant and a little shop where we're going, so all you'll really need is a change of clothes, something half warm, and a toothbrush," Boyd points out.

Roy sucks some air between his teeth. "All I'm taking is some chocolate and some other stuff we might need," he says defensively.

"Two backpacks is a lot of chocolate," I point out dryly.

This sets Roy off on a rich train of thought that involves how much chocolate we could manage to eat in a weekend. "It's all right, guys," he says at length. "I'll put one bag on the carrier and one on my back, and it will all be sweet."

In truth, neither Boyd nor I pushes the two-backpack issue too hard. Secretly, we're not all that unhappy about the handicap he's giving himself. I for one hate always being at the back all the time, and Boyd has a healthy competitive instinct that doesn't like being second every time.

Davy rides past. "Bike shop closed at twelve," he says, and keeps on riding.

I look at my watch, and Boyd looks at his. Roy doesn't even look remotely perturbed. He has a string-and-chewing-gum approach to solving problems, and somehow I know that all the bike bits strewn over the car park, the tube with its side wall blown out, and the two backpacks that against all advice he's still busily filling with stuff he might conceivably need on the weekend, will all magically come together, and we'll be off. I've seen it happen many times before, and rather than worry, my main interest is in seeing how Roy will make it all happen.

Roy's examining the original flat tube, to see if it can be fixed, when Davy pedals back along the road and throws two tubes from ten metres away.

"Bummed them off a couple of young kids I found riding their bikes around town," he says by way of explanation.

Roy, who always knows things will somehow work out, takes good fortune in his stride, and pumps up the tyre again, but more carefully this time. "Right then," he declares, and bounces the tyre on the bitumen.

Then, before I even have time to put on a pair of gloves and a helmet, the bike parts strewn over the car park come together. All the bits not coming with us are thrown back in the cars and, following the exciting scent of adventure, we're on the bikes and off chasing the already lowering sun.

The flat, undulating country out from Boonah gives little clue as to what awaits. With time tight, Boyd and Roy take turns out the front pushing things along, while Davy, bored at the pace, finds culverts and obstacles to jump over and through on the side of the road. We're an hour in when I realise things aren't well with Roy. He keeps shifting his weight on the bike and wriggling uncomfortably on the seat. For once, our normal roles are reversed, and I ride along beside him, observing what's happening. It soon becomes obvious that the bags are unbalancing him.

"Which is the heavier bag?" I enquire as we ride along.

Roy indicates the one on his back.

"Pull over, and we'll change them around, then," I say, enjoying the role reversal. I help him remove his backpack and almost drop it. It feels like it weighs twenty kilos. "What are these?" I ask, fingering the hard shapes that have been digging into his back and making him so uncomfortable.

"Just stuff," he says defensively.

"They feel like cans," I say.

"That'll be the baked beans," he says. "I threw a couple of tins in for breakfast."

"But we've told you there's a shop up there," Boyd points out again, but with less grace than the last time he visited the subject.

"We're away for three days, so we might get hungry," Roy insists.

We switch bags around, so he wears the lighter on his back, and he's immediately much more comfortable. Soon, despite the headwind, we're rattling along at a good pace.

The approaches to the first big climb are deceptive. We ride up a pretty, narrow, tree-filled valley which is only gently uphill. There is a vague sense of the valley sides closing in on us then, without warning, we change from dead flat to straight up. As soon as I realise this is the climb, I have one final go at the baked beans issue.

"Roy, there's a big rock over there. You could hide anything you don't need behind it, and we could recover it on the way back."

Roy, having lugged the weight this far, has locked himself into the folly. He hangs stubborn and declines the suggestion, so up we go, baked beans and all.

I've learnt there is only one way for me to ride a hill like this, and that is in granny gear, and off the saddle all the way. Boyd and Roy choose to stay sitting, and I take up position just behind them. As with all big hills, there's no point in looking up, so eyes fixed on the front wheel, I settle into the task. It only takes five minutes before I begin to feel it in the legs. I want to start wandering back and forth across the road to lessen the slope, but I also want to keep up with the other two, so I ignore the developing pain and just grit my teeth and pedal on. Roy and Boyd seem to be powering up the hill, as if it wasn't even hurting, leaving me hanging on the back, for dear life. However, I note that even Roy's chatter has stopped, and the three of us are riding up in silence. Davy has already taken off. He'll ride to the top, come back down and then do it all again. We grind away at the endless climb. An occasional car slows, engine straining and exuding a hot scorched radiator smell from the bonnet. The occupants have a long look at us, and the car continues its own struggle up the tight curves. Each passing car produces a short surge of pride-driven adrenaline, and I briefly stand on the pedals with renewed vigour, trying my best to appear as if I'm not ready to fall sideways at any moment. Before long, I'm having 'when will I stop' conversations with myself. After the next corner, I'll get off, I decide. Perhaps, though, if I stay on just half a minute longer, then Boyd will crack first, and I can stop with competitive honour intact. I begin to slip inexorably off the back. At first, it's just a few metres, but then another few. I make a renewed attempt at getting back on, but immediately slip back, only further this time.

Then suddenly, just as I finally decide I absolutely have to stop for a minute, Boyd's mobile rings. It rings once, then twice. I can see him look across at Roy, perhaps wondering about the protocols of answering mobile phones while climbing steep hills.

"Better answer it, I suppose," Boyd says.

"Yes, you'd better," Roy agrees much too quickly.

I struggle up to them and park a few metres further up the slope.

"Yes, we're definitely still coming," Boyd is saying. "We're on bicycles, you see, but I expect we'll definitely be there before dark."

We're in amongst the trees, in a magic place whose charms are much better appreciated on a bicycle rather than enclosed in a car. The low sun is lighting the treetops, the whistling wind making the topmost swaying branches dance. Enjoying the wild ambience of this place, I'm glad we've momentarily stopped.

"How about that. Isn't that something else!" Roy exclaims, taken by the incongruity of technology invading such a lonely, windswept place.

But much as I'd like to linger, I also know that with all big hills, the top will never come as quickly as I think and, in the shade of the mountain, it's difficult to know how much light is left. We won't get to the top leaning over the front of our bikes, so we keep moving. We're just about back into a climbing rhythm when the phone rings again. Before I stop, I give one more big push on the pedal, so as not to give back a single centimetre of hill.

"I'll have mine well done," Boyd says after a few moments.

I shut my eyes. He's sounding for all the world like he's just snapped shut the menu and is now about to have a friendly discussion around the table, when in reality we're battling the hill for all we're worth, operating at the edge of our physical limits and chasing the rapidly falling sun. I open my eyes again, back to the reality of the cold wind rattling the trees, in a wild and lonely place. Yet somehow the enquiries of civilized dining that Boyd now throws up the hill towards us, are a welcome, comforting intrusion into the grim task of subduing the hill.

"Pepper steak, well done," I answer him.

Roy thinks there must be something hugely funny here to explore, and we resume climbing with him expounding on the ridiculous and the surreal elements of the situation. However, the laughter lasts only a minute, and soon everyone's eyes drop again; We resume the grim, silent ascent. Soon, the need to stop begins to build in my legs and chest with an urgency that I can't ignore, but I also sense there's more wind on my face, and the trees are thinning. A view begins to appear on my right, and it dawns on me — we're at the top of the first climb.

We take a moment to enjoy the visual rewards on offer, and now that we're at the top, everyone can admit how hard they struggled. But with time and light not waiting at our discretion, we resume our chase of the sun. Maybe it's the relief of being back into undulating country, but Roy starts duelling with Davy, having races to the top of the next rise.

I try to reign in his enthusiasm. "There's another climb coming," I tell him, in the part-pleading, part-scolding, knowing voice of a parent who's being completely ignored. We seem to be on a wide plateau, and for a moment I wonder if my memory has deceived me, but when I see the lookout as a speck high up on our left, I know it will be just as bad as I remember. Unlike the first, the second climb starts off gently enough, but just as Roy's making not-nearly-as-bad-as-the-last noises, it kicks up viciously. We're losing the light, and there will be no support car to rescue me this time, so I've no alternative but to ignore my spent, trembling legs, and to climb for all I'm worth. I've retreated into my own world, just pushing one pedal then the other, when I become aware of a change in my surroundings. The usual grunting and tyre noises are missing. I ease back, barely turning the pedals over, waiting for wheels to appear. I try to throw a glance back down the road, but the corners are tight, and as far as I can tell, I'm on my own. I don't want to stop, because I know I might not be able to resume. Eventually, Davy rides up beside me. "Dad's got off," he says, and for a moment it's as if he's said that the world as we know it had just come to an end. "What! Is he ill or something?" I ask, thinking that nothing less than a heart attack would get him off the bike.

"No, he's just buggered, that's all."

I suggest to Davy that he rides back and swaps bikes with his dad, and see if that gets Roy to the top. Davy disappears back down the hill and soon reappears, pedalling the heavy bike with the bag on the back. Even super-fit Davy looks like he's working hard.

"I don't know how he rode it this far," Davy says with a touch of awe in his voice.

Then, as we ride along discussing the wider implications of Roy getting off the bike, the killer slope starts to ease, and I realise we've reached the top.

Davy and I ride out of the trees, into a beautiful crisp winter sunset. Mt. Superbus, one of Queensland's highest mountains, is framed on our right. We ride on slowly, waiting for the others to catch up, and a how-lucky-am-I feeling starts to overwhelm me. We're now exposed, riding straight into the teeth of a stiff westerly, and now that I'm not working so hard, the sweat soon feels like a coating of ice on my skin. Night is coming fast, and though I'd like to linger with this moment, we've still got ten kilometres or so before we make it in. Fortunately, it's a long slow drop down to Queen Mary Falls. All too quickly, the cold begins to seep properly through me, and soon I'm shivering. But the view and the day and the achievement of having conquered both hills, are all impacting me.

"Doesn't get much better than this," I say to Davy through chattering teeth, and the truth is, it probably won't.

Roy and Boyd finally catch us up, and we start a charge through the gathering dusk for the safety of the caravan park at the falls. It's a fast, no brakes descent through the rainforest, and the perfect reward for all the endless climbing. The day has finally gone, and I'm riding on trust, pointing the bike towards where the black in front of me is blackest. Any pothole, any stick on the road or even a sharp turn will make a perfect day end badly, but before we know it, the lights of the caravan park appear. As I ghost silently in, a line of formless dark shadows also pulls in behind me, the gentle crunching of gravel announcing we've all safely arrived.

Later I'm sitting on the steps of our cabin, freshly showered, and rugged up against the cold. The sign above the cabin's door says 'Daggs' after one of the nearby falls. It seems an appropriate name for the motley crew inside, and Boyd thinks that next time we do a mountain bike event at Kooralbyn, we should name our team 'The Daggs'.

I'm trying to work out how I'm feeling. My body is giving out signals of faint distress. My heart rate is still very much elevated, but given what I've just done, I'm feeling remarkably good. Someone in the next cabin strolls out into the night and lights up a cigarette. He's a man about my age.

"When did you get in?" he asks.

"Just on dark," I reply.

He nods as if calculating. "When we passed you, you guys weren't even halfway up the first hill."

"Yeah, we had to get a real wriggle on towards the end," I say with the cool air of someone who regularly does these sorts of things, and always has the situation under control.

"Was it a good ride up?" he asks.

“Yeah, we were out of the wind most of the way, and there was no heat stress, which tends to make all the difference,” I reply, avoiding the real thrust of his question. I like the way he’s looking at me. It’s a look of respect. It’s a wistful, wish-I-was-able-to-still-do-that look, and not one that thinks me crazy. I feel like I want to tell him that it wasn’t as hard a climb as it must appear to him. I want to tell him that if you learn the art of riding a bike very, very slowly, then even a seemingly endless steep hill, that even his car struggled to conquer, can’t beat you in the end.

Roy’s sitting at the kitchen table. The steaks were huge, and we’re well fed. Roy’s yawning between each sentence. It’s thirty-six hours since he last slept, yet his mind’s still racing. “Tomorrow, we’ll drop down the other side of the hill into Killarney. Boyd says you can come back up along the valley, and that will give us another go at that second hill that beat me today.”

I don’t want to even think of attempting that hill again, so I pick up a magazine Roy’s put on the bottom of my bed. It has ‘Epic’ on the cover. I start to flick through it. It’s all about a hundred-kilometre mountain bike event coming up.

“Two kilometres of vertical,” I say out loud. “That’s probably twice the climbing we’ve just done, today.” Two kilometres of vertical now has a meaning for me, and my legs completely understand the import of those words. "That's really hardcore stuff," I say, shaking my head in wonder. I start to calculate how long a ride like that would take me. I was lapping the gentle hills of Kooralbyn at about twelve kilometres an hour. That would mean it would take at least eight and a half hours. But I wouldn't be able to keep up that pace all day, so it would be even longer. I shake my head again. How could people contemplate putting themselves through that sort of torture?

Roy's unpacking his bag. The two cans of baked beans make their appearance and are sitting triumphantly on the table. Somehow, even then, I know they'll join us on the journey back down the mountain. A big old battery, weighing a least a kilogram, emerges and lands heavily beside them.

"Thought we might get to go for a night ride," Roy says before I ask.

I'm eagerly watching for what else might appear, so at first, I don't pick up what he says next.

"The reason I thought we'd better get a ride like this in, is we needed to have done some serious, serious hills before we attempt the Epic."

It takes a few seconds to take in what he's just said, then my jaw drops.

"Of course, you might think of getting yourself a new bike before we do it, something with suspension; be pretty hard otherwise."

There is no point in arguing, though. The word 'no' doesn't manage to disturb the air between us simply because the many ways the brain can formulate that simple word trip over each as they clamber to rush out. But by then it's too late as Roy's head has already slipped sideways, and he's sound asleep, still sitting in the chair.

CHAPTER 5
THE REAL THING (EPIC 1)

Once they complete their first Grand Tour, professional bike riders say that the experience of riding long stages, day after day for three whole weeks, changes their physiology completely and permanently. It is as if the sustained effort over that length of time triggers a response in the body that says, 'well that is what we do every day, so we'd better make the kind of changes that allow that to happen more easily.' A pale reflection of this bodily reaction will happen to any of us undertaking any level of exercise. The key to making it happen, though, is in the regularity of the exercise. As long as the activity is something we do most days, the body will respond by trying to deliver the kind of body we need to perform that activity. This is the case, no matter our age or level of fitness.

The question remains, though, and needs to be asked, whether older bodies and older hearts can keep up sustained high-grade effort over a long time. When I first got back on the bike and I used to ride it to work, there was a short steepish hill early on in the route. As I started on that hill, I often thought, *surely my heart can't keep doing this day after day,* and there was a nagging fear in the background that it would somehow wear out from the effort involved.

This fear was also fed by the night a few years before, that I'd spent in the coronary care unit of the hospital, and the subsequent treadmill test I'd had to terminate early, due to rhythm abnormalities. The fear of underlying heart disease was something I then carried around, as an underground, nagging weight.

I want to focus on that fear of exercise for a page or two, and examine the whole idea of risk. Hopefully, I've already started you down the track of dispelling the notion that exercise is something that strains old hearts and is, therefore, to be avoided.

Hopefully, you're taking on board the message that old heart muscle responds well to being worked. However, is this true for people with existing heart or artery disease, or other pre-existing heart conditions? It is a sad truth that none of us will have completely got away with things. We all have to pay the piper for the way we have lived. Given western diet and lifestyles, most people will reach middle age with some degree of artery disease. The question then becomes, how should we let this fact influence and inform our views on exercise? Most books of this type might be expected to carry careful advice to 'please consult your doctor before undertaking any exercise program.' Consider the warning duly given. There is a small risk of heart attack when sedentary people first engage in high-level exercise. However, think for a moment about what that means. If you were to take the exercise plunge, and on the first day you took the stairs instead of the lift, and halfway up you suffered a heart attack, then the truth is you were probably going to have that heart attack anyway. Perhaps not that day, but in the very near future. The advanced disease was there already, and all you would likely have done would be to bring forward the timing. Exercise is something we should absolutely ease into, hastening slowly, and building on gradually through time. However, the last thing people with known heart disease should do is become a 'cardiac cripple', fearful of any activity. In the end, the truth is that inactivity will only further exacerbate the problem that it fears.

The principle that muscle anywhere in the body will respond well to being worked also applies also to hearts with significant artery disease. Not only will muscle quality improve, but the blood supply also will improve. This is partly because all through our bodies, there are little vessels called collaterals. These small interconnecting channels between arteries are found throughout the vascular tree. For instance, if plaque completely blocks the single major artery in your leg, the leg doesn't turn black and fall off. Blood finds a way past the obstruction via these small collateral channels. Were your leg unsuitable for bypass surgery, you would not be advised to rest the limb. Rather, you would be advised to exercise as much as you could within the limits of pain. The body's response to working that limb hard would be to open up and enlarge the interconnecting collaterals to maximise the blood supply to the leg, as well as forming new blood vessels.

Not having perfect heart arteries moving into old age might be a legacy we carry. But if we understand the body's response to muscles with compromised blood supply, we will be much less fearful of exercising our hearts. If we do have a heart attack at some point, the chances of survival or of minimizing damage to heart muscle often will depend on the quality of the collateral channels within our hearts. These collaterals tend to open up and become of better quality in response to work. Therefore, the 'vascular conditioning' that exercise produces, and which has a protective effect on the heart, will be greater, and the chances of surviving and/or minimizing the damage from a heart attack will be improved, and not lessened, by exercise.

Sedentary people will often point to other types of risk involved with exercise such as bike riding; for instance, the physical risk of falling off your bike or being hit by a car. Sitting on the couch carries none of these risks, of course, but is still by far the riskier option. With the couch option, the risk is silent, creeping and ultimately deadly. For every person picked up by an ambulance on the side of the road having been knocked off their bike, many, many more arrive in hospital as victims of inactivity and the silent killers — stroke and heart attack. In the risk-to-benefit assessment of exercise when compared to sitting on the couch, there is a clear winner as to where risk really lies.

Returning now to the fear my heart would give out if I continued to ride that hill. The low-grade fear continued until the day I turned my thinking around completely and saw things from the proper perspective. I began to understand that my heart, rather than wearing out, was becoming rejuvenated and renewed by the daily work. We all need to arrive at this way of thinking. Ageing hearts do not need to be rested; they need to be worked harder, and will become all the healthier if we do. The image of older persons sitting around drinking tea and being delicate and inactive is a self-fulfilling, self-perpetuating image. If we buy into it, it won't be long before our shoulders become more rounded and we settle into the hunched shuffle of the old. The truth is that exercise-promoted heart health becomes more important with age, not less, and we need to be out there doing more and not less of the stuff that will keep hearts healthy.

I read and re-read the course information for the Epic. Descriptions of 'speeds approaching 100 kph coming down the Devil's Tail,' are meant to excite me, but all I feel is scared and apprehensive. It talks of exhilarating, steep, single track descents. When my fertile imagination combines that with the magnificent, unsurpassed views it describes from the top of the climbs, I see myself traversing narrow technical paths with cliffs on one side and thousand-foot sheer drops on the other, awaiting my any mistake. Worse than the thought of actually falling, though, is the thought that I'll be halfway down a descent and freeze, unable to go forward or back.

I phone up Roy in a panic of insecurity. He's reassuring.

"There's nothing that bad," he says.

But I pick up a brief hesitation between 'nothing' and 'bad'. "How bad, then, is not that bad?" I ask, gripping the phone hard and listening intently, as if my life depends on his reply.

"Nothing you won't be able to handle," he says, obtusely, and I swallow hard. "Listen," he says with soothing confidence. "You've done the work. That ride up to Queen Mary Falls will have hardened your legs for all the climbing. You got yourself around the Kooralbyn track without falling off too many times, so you're technically there or thereabouts, and you've already done one hundred kilometres on the road so your legs will have distance in them. You're ready for this."

I've heard this coaxing, sweet-talking, we-can-paddle-the-canoe-over-the-falls-and-nothing-bad-will-happen voice many times, and my rational mind knows not to believe him. However, I've rung him up precisely because I want to hear a reassuring voice.

"They reckon one hundred kilometres on dirt is worth two hundred on the road," I point out in token dissent.

"Well, you did that extra twenty into my place, so you're not that far short," he answers dismissively, as if in the abstract world of numbers two hundred and one hundred were close enough so that the difference didn't matter.

"It's a good entry-level machine," my local bike shop man, Paul, says reassuringly. "All the important components are of that middle range quality that won't fall apart on you." I trust Paul. He's old school — straight and honest, there to inform as much as to sell.

He does a circuit around the bike, wiping his hands on an oily rag before grabbing the handlebars. "See these front forks," he says, pushing down hard to demonstrate the point. "These aren't those toy, pretend, front suspensions you see around, these are the real thing." He bends down low, reading something on the rear derailleur. "Have a look yourself, that derailleur isn't rubbish, either." Then he straightens up to give me a what-more-will-it-take-to-convince-you look, before adding, "And, of course, you've got the disc brakes into the bargain."

"Then how come it's so cheap?" I ask.

"Well, the price of bikes has been coming steadily down," he replies as if he can't believe it himself. "You get a lot of bike for your money, these days, and this is a good all-round solid bike."

It's the word 'solid' that finally sells it. To me, that word has only positive connotations. I pick it up and feel its 'solid' weight, and the sheer heaviness of the bike is somehow reassuring as if it will help anchor me to terra firma. I'm thinking that even if my knees should give out soon, or if for some other reason my two-wheeling enthusiasm suddenly diminishes, at this price I still can't go wrong.

Paul is open late on Thursdays, and I ride my new bike back to the car through near-deserted streets. Tentatively, I ride over the edge of the kerb to see how the newly-acquired suspension works. I'm expecting shuddering of my forearms, but it never happens. I try it again to see if I'd imagined the smooth transition from footpath to road. Soon I'm like any other teenager, up on the pedals, slipping on and off the footpath. It takes me half an hour to reach the car, as I ride around the darkened streets looking for kerbs, and other obstacles to drop down off, all the time savouring this new magic that is front suspension.

The next day I ride my shining new machine down the hill near home, over some rough ground heading towards the creek.

The suspension smooths out all the jolting bumps, and it finally dawns on me why everyone passed me, not only when I was riding up the Kooralbyn hills, but also when I shuddered my way down the slopes.

I practise riding my new suspension bike on the rutted ground of the cane fields. To get to them, I ride down the hill and cross the creek via a small open wooden bridge. At the top of the hill, I let go of the brakes and imagine I'm hurtling down the Devil's Tail at one hundred kilometres per hour. One day, on the lead-up to the Epic, a gentle rain is falling. I reach the bridge, dodge a puddle, and line up my new bike crookedly on the bridge planks. Suddenly, the word 'wet' jumps alarmingly into my brain, and my fingers instinctively reach for the brakes at the same time my front wheel meets the wet sheen of wood.

The very next moment, I'm looking at running water, and when I swing around I'm examining the underside of the bridge, only to return to a study of the gently rippling creek. It takes a few seconds to work out that my legs are still entangled with the bike and are holding me from dropping into the water. The bike, in turn, has stayed entangled with the bridge, suspended half on and half off. I hang there while I establish that I'm substantially in one piece, with my legs sending out only stinging bruised signals, then I slowly turn the world the right way up, haul myself back up onto the bridge and disentangle my legs. I hobble and skip my way through the worst of the hurting, and slowly the eye-watering sharpness of the pain recedes. The bike turns out to be undamaged, but the message is imprinted indelibly in my brain, in the way that only pain can truly do — danger, wet wood is slippery. I'm still on the steepest of learning curves, and the Epic is only weeks away. There must be a hundred other situations I've not yet encountered on a mountain bike. There will undoubtably be a thousand places where a novice like me could come to grief over the hundred-kilometre event but strangely, though these concerns are real enough, they are fighting a losing battle with the increasingly warm anticipation of a great adventure.

The Epic is an annual mountain bike event which used to start at a winery just south of Toowoomba and finish near Grandchester, not far from Ipswich. The hills and valleys all through that country tend to be orientated north-south, but we will be riding west-east across them. The ups will be long and often, the downs will be steep, and for me, scary.

On the afternoon before the event, we turn up to register and familiarize ourselves with the start. Wives have been co-opted as support crew and encouragers. Because we find ourselves at a winery, we all end up sitting around a table lazily enjoying the warm spring afternoon, sipping at cool drinks and enjoying the ambience of an idyllic setting. Nevertheless, I know this seeming perfection is illusory, and the reality is that, come morning, this peaceful place will be transformed into a pre-battle staging area, and I'll be going over the top, with no guarantee I'll survive the coming day. However, the longer I sit in the sun, enjoying the company of friends, and listening to Roy tell racing stories, the more my trepidation is reduced to a low background hum, and I feel an overarching sense of privilege settle over me. In under a year, I've gone from being unable to even ride the gentle hills around my place, to being amongst the ranks of the fortunate few attempting a mountain bike marathon up and over the Great Dividing Range.

Early spring's daytime temperatures are rapidly warming, but nights up on the Darling Downs remain cool. Staying with Boyd's brother, we enjoy country hospitality, overlooking the flat farming plains of the Downs. We savour special, wide landscapes of endless space, and smooth horizons which fill the eye with a vastness broken only by the button of an occasional flat-topped distant hill. It's a particularly jolly evening with us free to consume copious amounts of food in the guise of stoking up for the coming day.

I take some time out and ask Davy to check my new bike.

"You sure that's the height you want the seat?" he asks in a tone that suggests there's something strange in not having your backside higher than your head.

"It's my back Davy," I reply, with a one-day-you-too-will-be-old sigh. "I like to sit kind of very upright."

He bounces around the driveway, getting a feel for the bike. "Nice bike," he says diplomatically.

I wait expectantly as he flicks the gear levers up and down and tests the brakes. Davy's been winning races all year, and even though he's still very young, his opinions already have the weight of an ace rider attached to them. "I don't know if you want the brake levers way up here, though," he points out with polite concern. "You really need to have the brakes where your fingers can get to them quickly."

I show him just how quickly my fingers can shoot forward and find the brakes. "Again, I suppose it's just a matter of always being used to having them up here," I say, clinging to the familiar.

A cross between pity and fear enters his eyes. "That's well and good if you're riding on the flat, but as soon as you're up on the pedals and you go to drop down into some steep gully, then what happens is your hands naturally roll forward on the grips, and if the brakes are way up high like this, you'll end up having to cock your wrists to reach them."

I look at the way only his thumbs are left gripping the handlebars, and renewed visions of me somersaulting my way down a hillside saunter unfiltered across the worst of the mind's inventions.

"Better put them down just a bit, then," I quickly agree.

At least Boyd is also nearly as raw as I am. Apart from Kooralbyn, this is also his first mountain bike event. We prod at each other's tyres seeking enlightenment.

"Mine are a lot softer," he says, looking at me to justify why the discrepancy exists.

I scratch my head. I've a vague notion that pedalling with hard tyres involves less effort, and therefore, hard must be better. "I put more air in, because they'll roll better, and because if they're too soft, you run the danger of pinch flats," I pronounce, sounding believable, but merely parroting someone else's wisdom.

"But you'll have less control in the soft stuff," Boyd counters, and succeeds in pressing the right button.

In the end, he puts a bit more air in, and I let some out.

Roy walks by and gives my tyres a squeeze. "Way too soft," he says.

I put the air back in, but then I picture myself sliding out in a turn and continuing over a cliff edge, so I sneak some air out again. That night, I take a while to drop off to sleep, apprehension keeping my mind buzzing. Eventually, though, I do drift off, with my twitching limbs still riding the Devil's Tail.

Like the rising sun scattering a fog, morning dissolves the tossing anxieties of night. The house is all business and laughing excitement from the moment it wakes. I've worked out I'll probably be eight hours in the saddle at best, but more likely nine, so I've bought myself a pair of nicks, as I'll need all the padded assistance I can muster. I've also bought a fair dinkum riding shirt with pockets in the back to store food. I walk around with an unfamiliar tightness tugging at my thighs, and a new-shirt feel on my back, busily working my way through a checklist of things I need to do. Lingering at the breakfast table socializing with our hosts, Roy is still making no real progress towards organizing himself. I can hear Boyd in the background, beginning to give him regular time calls. I've just about got everything in order when Boyd starts the 'we're-out-of-here' countdown and moves towards the front door. This finally makes

Roy pay attention, and he starts circling the lounge searching for far-scattered gear.

"Has anyone seen my front wheel?" he asks. Boyd pivots at the door.

"Only joking," Roy says, but not quickly enough to avoid a shoulder punch.

As the sun breaks over the wide horizon, the bikes are thrown on to the back of the cars, Boyd makes Roy check that every item of equipment has found its way into the car, and we're off.

In the morning cool, we join the mass of bikes milling around the start area. I wonder if my new bike and I look the part, or whether I stand out as an obvious fraud, with new nicks and shirt, and the new, too-polished sheen of the bike marking me indelibly as a first-timer, and object of pity. As the start time approaches, I ride around warming my legs, and with a good, ready-to-go tightness in my stomach. Boyd, suddenly gripped by indecision, decides to head back to the car to put more air in his tyres. I think about doing the same, but above all else, I want these tyres to stick to the track, so I leave mine on the soft side.

Boyd returns just in time for the final countdown. "Remember," he says as we line up, "this will be a long day, so there's no need to hurry."

The starter sends us off, and I let myself enjoy the spectacle of bobbing heads and colourful shirts elongate up the first hill. I give the wives a confident wave as I pass, and aim to slowly ease my way up the hill. Roy's already chasing hard at the front, and I won't see him again till day's end, but then I notice Boyd is also already halfway up the hill and going hard. Inwardly groaning, I start to chase up towards him through the closely-packed bikes. In an excitement of wrong gears, I lose my chain and have to chase even harder to catch up. He's pedalling as if the finish was just over the next hill, and I'm soon on my limit just trying to keep him in sight. Eventually, I catch up and we turn off the road down a narrow dirt track. The mass of bicycles is strung out into two lines following tracks that tractor tyres have made, and I find myself on a long, shallow, fast, downhill run. I'm concentrating hard, because everyone is still tightly packed, and it won't just be me I take out if I fall. I give myself a fright when I go too fast into a sharp corner, and it's all I can do to hold things together and not follow a set of skid marks which have already headed bush this morning. I give myself a mental slap on the wrist. I don't want this day to end just fifteen minutes in.

We're soon on a section of single track, and I come to a steep-sided gully. Some people are riding down into it, others are walking. “I ride gullies like this, don’t I?” I ask myself at the top of the drop. That’s the trouble when you’re a novice and have minimal experience to inform your choices. In the end, I take a breath, ride down, and launch myself at the other side. Once out of the gully, the hill keeps going up and is too steep to ride, so I join everyone else in walking.

Boyd’s waiting at the top. “So far so good,” he says, sucking away at his water bottle.

“So far, it is,” I agree.

We’ve come nearly ten kilometres, and as Roy said, it’s nothing I can’t handle. Just as we start moving again, we turn through a gate and down a technical set of rocky steps, taking me right out of my comfort zone. I hold on white-knuckled tight and make it to the bottom. The rapid descent down into Ma Ma creek is about to begin.

The tightly-bunched field has not yet begun to spread out, and I can feel the pressure of all the bikes behind me. As much as I’d like to pick my way slowly, I know this is not the time. So I latch on to the wheel in front, and the next twenty minutes turns into a series of what-happens-when revelations. “Right, so that’s what happens when you go over a drop-off like that at speed,” I say to myself, as I stay locked onto the wheel in front. At a mad, exhilarating pace, I roll on over rough and smooth, not thinking for myself, not questioning, but learning fast by simply following closely whatever the bike in front is doing. Eventually, we reach the creek, the slope levels out and my heart slows.

The near fifteen kilometre run along the creek is special — full of dry, fast, single track, crossing and re-crossing the creek. It's what mountain biking is all about. I'm following a female rider down into a rock-strewn creek crossing when she suddenly brakes hard. I'm close up behind and have to do the same, and I end up pitching forward onto the bike stem. It's an eye-watering injury, and for a minute I think I've damaged myself significantly. But after sitting by the side of the track for a few minutes, the pain goes and I ride on, albeit subdued. The mad pace of the first few kilometres has long gone, Boyd's disappeared up ahead, the field is more spread, and I settle in to enjoying the warm embrace of the bush and the exhilaration of negotiating the thin, dusty, ribbon of track that will stretch out enjoyably before me well into the late afternoon.

Boyd's waiting at the first stop. "What did you think of that?" he asks, a ruddy glow of enjoyment visible under the sweat.

"As good as it gets," I reply. We're a couple of hours into the event, and only a quarter of the way there, and I'm already weary and overdue for this stop. I'm also totally enjoying myself.

After the first checkpoint, we begin to climb and keep climbing. Boyd stays with me for a while, then slowly pulls away. I let him go. I'm beginning to feel it in the legs, but at least in climbing, I'm in familiar territory. I settle back and keep my eyes on the front wheel. Half an hour later, my reward is the view from the top of the Razorback. I spend a few minutes taking it in, then start the descent. In the lead up to the race, the profile of the track showed an almost vertical descent from the Razorback. I'd imagined it would be scary and way beyond my technical limits, but I manage to negotiate the steep rutted track without incident, and even feel a stab of disappointment when I reach the bottom.

As we exit onto the road below, someone says, "That's the last of the single track for a while," and I feel myself relax. I've survived the creek, been down the steepest and roughest descent of the day and so far, I've stayed intact. My head lifts, and I breathe in the cool mountain air. This is the most fun I've had for many a day. The halfway stop is only fifteen kilometres up the road, with only the Devil's Tail in between to worry over.

On the next major climb, my legs start to seriously complain, and I allow myself a celebratory stop at the top to regroup and rest them. At least I now know I'll make it to the half-way point. The Devil's Tail turns out to be an enjoyable anticlimax. It's merely fast, wind-in-the-hair fun, with just a sting in the tail where we transition from bitumen to dirt at the bottom, and the back of the bike starts to wander disconcertingly in the loose gravel.

I'm tired but exhilarated when I reach the halfway, and I'm even beginning to believe I can do this. As they ply me with food, I garble on to the support crew about how good it was. They tell me Davy went through with the leaders, Roy's long gone and Boyd's just left. I'm torn between staying and resting for a while, or not falling too far behind. Adrenaline's still flowing in my veins and the sugar lift is making me feel good, so I leave as quickly as good manners will allow and, refreshed and in high spirits, start off along the valley floor.

I stare at the front tyre, disbelieving, hoping it always looked this flat. It doesn't appear to be deflating quickly, so I stop, blow it up again and hope it stays hard. However, it only takes a few kilometres, and it's flat once more. I stop, unpack my spare tube and busy myself changing it over. It's only a minor setback, and in the context of the day, I'll only lose five minutes. However, try as I might, I can't blow air into the new tube. A young fellow I had a yarn with as we rode into checkpoint two, stops to see if I need help. I try his pump, but the tube still refuses to inflate. Deciding the valve must be defective, I put the old tube back in and blow it up as hard as I can. I figure that if I can coax a couple of good kilometres out of each pump, then I'll only have to do this twenty more times before the finish. My preoccupation has now changed from how my quickly tiring legs are going to make it to the finish, to how I'll manage to nurse the bike home. I'm now somewhere near the back of the field, and in a position to see evidence of the toll this race is taking. There are still forty kilometres to go, and the sun's on the way down. The light-hearted enjoyment so evident earlier in the race, is gradually giving way to discomfort and fatigue. I'm passing slow-moving people who have 'struggle' written all over their faces. I'm meeting people parked by the side of the track, flexing their cramped muscles. For my part, though increasingly weary, and with the focus well and truly changed to survival and challenge, I'm still greatful to be out here 'doing stuff'.

Somewhere along the track, I notice I hadn't done up the zip on my little tool bag under the saddle, and all my tools, apart from a single tyre lever, have fallen out. But it doesn't dent my upbeat mood. I'm still moving forward, the pump's still working, the kilometres are coming down, and at least the bike is now lighter.

I struggle to the top of Laidley Gap and tick it off the list. According to the map profile, it's the last of the big climbs, and I pump the front tyre up as hard as I can for the long descent. For some reason, the description of this descent as being both fast and technical has caused me the most sleeplessness. But I've been six hours in the saddle, and something strange has happened. The bike and I have bonded, and I feel perfectly safe as I launch myself down the other side of the Gap. For the first time ever on a mountain bike, I feel totally in control, with not a single doubt that I'll make it down in one piece.

I wander into the last of the checkpoints. A great weariness is settling over me, as I go about the business of filling water bottles and scrounging the last of the food. I find someone with a decent upright pump in the back of their car and blow the tyre up as hard as I dare. I figure I've at least saved myself three sessions with the hand pump, and in the strange psychology of exhaustion, it's a major victory. Leaving the checkpoint, I tell myself that twenty-odd more kilometres is not far, and all the big climbs are behind me.

There's a fellowship of encouragement at the back of the field. All the non- athletes, the less well prepared and the old like me, are well represented amongst those I find along the track. Pushing the bike up to the top of Edward's Gap, I talk to an exhausted middle-aged woman, who's not making much forward progress. She looks totally out on her feet, but as I talk to her, it becomes apparent she's already decided she'll get to the end, even if her body has long since disagreed with the decision. I ride on, and somehow I know I'll see her cross the finish line. I'm beginning to be thankful to Roy for the conditioning of the Queen Mary Falls ride. My legs are very tired but, so far, there are no cramps. I'm into my routine — pedal a few kilometres, pump up the tyre, pedal a few more. I pass and then am re-passed by the same weary people at each tyre-pumping stop. Every little hill is now a serious trial, and braking has become a dispensable option as I eke out every last centimetre of energy-saving uphill roll at the end of each downhill charge.

The young fellow who unsuccessfully lent me his pump rolls past as I yet again blow up my tyre. He tells me he doesn't think he can make it, but I tell him, 'Of course you will, and I'll see you at the finish.' I now know that I'll get there, though every kilometre is becoming harder. Helpfully, an official tells us there are only five kilometres to go. He's trying to be encouraging, but doesn't he realise five kilometres is a huge distance? I go through periods of great weariness and periods where I'm back having a great experience, but the periods of weariness are beginning to run together. I think of blowing my tyre up one last time, but I decide I'm well and truly over pumping up tyres for today. It can stay flat, even if I end up riding home on the rim. I meet someone lying by the track, both legs cramped and solid. I ask him if there's anything I can do, but he shakes his head and motions for me to keep going.

On a perfectly straight part of the track, the bike in front suddenly wobbles, falls on its side and slides down the steep little hill the track is traversing. I stop till the rider scrambles back up the slope with the bike. He's as bemused as I am as to why it happened. The sun is beginning to disappear, my tyre is nearly fully flat, and I'm on automatic pilot. I stop asking myself how far, and concentrate on making fifty metres, then another fifty. Then, just as I'm about to accuse every race official I've ever met of being total liars, I look up, and there are tents up ahead. A surge of adrenaline lifts my legs, making the last few hundred metres seem as easy as the first few hundred of the day.

I find Boyd and fall on the grass beside him, weary but exhilarated. We're near the finish line so I can clap everyone else home. Food and drink are thrust into my hands, and congratulations offered. I clap in the young fellow who tried to lend me his pump, and the middle-aged lady, as she literally falls over the line. Soon exhaustion gives way to a warm sense of elation, and the highlights of the day begin to form in my head for endless enjoyable replay.

Roy appears freshly showered, with no visible evidence of the day's effort. "Hey,

you made it in," he says loudly, but with a measure of relief in his voice.

I raise myself up onto one elbow. "Sorry, I've made everyone wait," I say.

"You're not lookin' too bad, you know," he says, with some evident surprise.

"No, it's all good. I'm feeling just great," I say, as a sudden movement makes my leg cramp.

"So, you didn't have too many dramas out there?" he asks, guiltily.

"No, none, nothing I couldn't handle, anyway. Perfect day, really."

"You know what's really good about today?" he asks rhetorically.

"No," I say.

"You're finally there!"

"Yep, it's good we all made it safely in."

"No, I mean you're there -you've finally arrived. You've done all the hard work, and from now on, till we turn sixty, it's all just going to be so much fun."

CHAPTER 6
ALL NIGHT LONG

It's time to explore the other great cause of plaque being deposited on artery walls. Previously, I used the analogy of the sediment-laden river to help you understand how plaque is deposited. Now I'd like to extend the analogy. So far, the analogy would suggest that plaque deposition is accelerated in situations where the sediment load in the blood is high (high cholesterol levels), or when slow, or eddy-rich disturbed flow, is present. The first situation is addressed by diet and/or cholesterol-lowering drugs. The second is addressed by stirring up the blood and making it regularly flow faster, through regular moderate exercise.

Now I'd like to introduce the third main factor — the 'stickiness' of the inner artery wall. In a river, you will find no sediment deposited on smooth rock, and in the same way, no cholesterol will stick to smooth, undamaged, artery walls. Understanding that simple proposition will help you understand why smokers, diabetics, and those with high blood pressure have significantly higher rates of cardiovascular disease.

The numerous toxic chemicals in cigarette smoke irritate and inflame the artery walls of smokers, and inflamed arteries are inherently more 'sticky'. The damaged walls not only allow cholesterol molecules to stick, but also make it easier for cholesterol to permeate this damaged inner vessel lining and form the plaque deposits. This happens to everyone who smokes. The official statistics might say that a smoker is, say, three times more likely to have a stroke than a non-smoker or five times more likely to have a heart attack, but in some ways, such statements can be misleading. They are not to be understood in a yes/no fashion as to whether or not a smoker has artery disease. All smokers sustain damage, and whether a smoker has a stroke or a heart attack is more a result of where plaque is deposited in the vessel and whether it is laid down in an even fashion or heaped up on the artery wall.

The biochemistry of a diabetic's blood is complex, but the end result is somewhat the same as smokers. Substances in the blood of chronic diabetics produce a chronic inflammatory response in the wall of their arteries, making them more 'sticky'. In a sobering thought for the rest of us, many people now postulate that the high sugar diets with their frequent sugar 'hits' of the non-diabetic population also set up a mild chronic inflammation in arteries. This might help explain the epidemic rates of vascular disease even in the general non-diabetic public.

High blood pressure (hypertension) represents a double whammy. It can be seen as the heart's response to increased resistance to blood flow. The heart is designed to function best within a narrow pressure range. The heart muscle in chronic high blood pressure states becomes thicker and the internal chamber size of the left ventricle, smaller. However, that kind of heart muscle is inherently stiffer, and as we've previously seen, stiff muscle is bad for the pump's operation.

It is also easy to grasp why high blood pressure is bad for artery health. It works this way. Greater resistance to blood flow through the arteries will happen in the following circumstances;

through them becoming stiffer pipes; through narrowing of the internal space by plaque build-up; through the wall becoming rough and inflamed. In the last circumstance, think of the inner wall surface offering more resistance by becoming more like sandpaper rather than glass. If the arteries offer more resistance to flow, the body will compensate by increasing the pump pressure, and high blood pressure will develop. For the same flow rate, the left ventricle might now have to pump with 160 mmHg., rather than the 120 mmHg. it formally generated. The artery walls do not like this increased pressure, and it causes further vessel wall damage. This damage, in turn, promotes more plaque to be deposited, and the damaged vessels to become harder, stiffer, pipes. All of which, of course, cause an even greater resistance to flow. Therefore, to keep the same volume circulating, a further increase in pressure becomes necessary, and on and on the spiral process goes, with blood pressure slowly increasing year-on-year-on-year. This is the reason doctors are so vigilant in checking blood pressure. High blood pressure is bad for heart muscle and bad for arteries.

To act against these promoters of artery wall damage, we have exercise. Exercise will not only decrease bad cholesterol, decrease blood pressure, and cause metabolic changes which allow the body to process sugar more efficiently. One of the ways it decreases blood pressure, is the way it benefits arteries at the cellular level. On the inside of the artery wall, exercise stimulates the production of vessel-repairing good chemicals such as nitrous oxide. At this cellular level, artery health is a dynamic process of continuous damage and repair, and exercise stimulates the production of new, healthy, wall-lining cells. In terms we might find easier to understand, the body has inbuilt ways of facilitating the delivery of the kind of blood supply we ask of it. At the level of the interface between blood and artery wall, exercise is the main anti-inflammatory vessel lining weapon which counters all the pro-inflammatory problems we inflict on ourselves.

Promotion of artery health at the cellular level is, probably, the biggest contribution exercise makes in fighting cardiovascular disease. None the less, I find the notion of stirring up the river sediment to be far more motivating and more psychologically satisfying. However, whatever are the complex mechanisms involved, we know that exercise is the main weapon we have in the fight. It is at least as effective as cholesterol-lowering drug therapies (statins) in preventing death from heart disease, and has the advantage, that while drugs only address the sediment load, exercise addresses the underlying problem.

However, when contemplating serious exercise, it is not the wonderful things you would be doing to benefit the inside lining of your blood vessels that occupies your mind; No, it's contemplation of the fun to be had, that fully occupies your thoughts.

I abandon the cross-table conversation, go quiet and concentrate on peeling prawns. My eyes drift slowly down to the plate in front of me, but my attention moves along to the conversation at the end of the table. Roy has moved in and is sitting seductively close. I don't even need to hear the exchange to know what's happening. An occasional glance up the table confirms he's laying on the smiling buddy-buddy talk, thick and irresistible. He'll ease his way in with some harmless small talk — a little punch to the shoulder, the laughing-oh-so-reasonable voice gradually ingratiating itself. Then, when the guard finally drops, he'll pounce. I know how he operates. He's done the same thing to me too many times to mention.

"Be strong, Boyd," I mutter to myself as I crack a crab shell in two. "Just say 'no', like we agreed this afternoon." Boyd's a barrister. He's no pushover. For the moment, he's leaning back in his seat, a wine glass cupped loosely in his hand, looking over his glasses in his best lawyer manner, firmly in control of the situation. He'll be able to argue our agreed position better than anyone. I turn away telling my aching legs not to worry, but unease lingers on. The wine bottle in front of Boyd is nearly empty.

It's been a good holiday. The kind that, afterwards, needs two full days set aside to catch up on sleep and let the body recover. We've given the canoes a good wetting, and this year didn't bend a single one around a boulder. The pushbikes have been unleashed — knobblies last week on the dirt roads of the canoe country around northern New South Wales, and the road bikes all this week. Tonight, we're sitting on the verandah of the Mapleton Hotel, with a panoramic view over the Sunshine Coast. We last scooted past here yesterday. We were on the bikes, then, sitting up, the hard work done, salivating over the red sign up ahead, 'STEEP DESCENT, TRUCKS USE LOW GEAR'. But now the holiday's nearly over, and tonight is the time for old friends to sit back, pleasantly weary and mellow together.

When I look over again at Boyd, the ambience of the moment evaporates. I take in the white knuckles wrapped around the wine glass stem, and the tell-tale retreat behind a helpless fixed grimace. A desperate begging eye wanders down the table in my direction. I frown and nod back encouragement, but his shoulders have already begun to slump, and I know there is nothing I can do to turn things around. It's all but over, and Roy, as usual, has won the day. I look away, unable to watch the inevitable capitulation.

Two days later, I get the call. "Boyd for you," my wife says as I accelerate down the corridor, taking refuge in the toilet in a vain attempt to escape the inevitable. I listen to the laughing exchanges in the corridor outside, groaning in anticipation of the coming conversation. My legs are still complaining, stressing their need for a few more days of restoration, but there's no avoiding my fate. I reluctantly open the door, and slowly shuffle my way into the corridor.

"Hello Boyd," I say with bright hopeless enthusiasm.

"It's on," he apologises, and waits to be hit.

I sigh but don't argue. If it's been decided, then everyone understands I'll fall into line. My weary body can protest all it likes, but my head has already moved past acceptance and onto practicalities.

"I haven't bought any lights," I say. "What do you reckon — one on the helmet, or one on the front of the bike?"

"I'd be doing both," Boyd replies.

"I'd like to get there in daylight, and ride some of the course," I say.

"If we can, I'd be for seeing the whole course in the daylight," Boyd agrees. "We're going to need all the help we can get."

I put the phone down and ponder the 'why' question. Arguably, it all fits broadly into Roy's 'fitter-at-sixty-than-fifty-philosophy', but a twelve-hour race beginning at dusk and extending all through the night until dawn, surely can't be good for ageing bodies. At least that's how Boyd and I saw things a few days ago. But, somehow, when Roy weaves an argument, the very fabric of reality is twisted. What is obvious madness ends up sounding entirely reasonable, and something not to be missed. In Roy's authorized version, sleep is the sole preserve of wimps, and an unnecessary intrusion into having fun. Health and fitness will be wonderfully enhanced by the occasion, and because this perfect opportunity may never come again, we should absolutely seize it with both hands and eagerly embrace this once-in-a-lifetime event. There are a few splinters of truth in this version, and it's not as if Boyd and I are unaware of the true effects of sleep deprivation when combined with intense physical activity. Yet, such are the devious, strange workings of my subconscious, that when I put the phone down, the mere thought of racing across a tree-littered hillside in the dead of night sends an immediate pulse of excitement smiling through my veins. Perhaps, the truth always was that we'd hoped Roy would overrule all the sensible objections and give us a rationale to spend the night breathless and sweaty. Notwithstanding the cautious dictates of common sense, and the combined sagging weight of our hundred-and-fifty-plus years, the glint in our eyes exists because we know something hidden from sensible people. For us, the attraction of simple, unwashed fun remains gloriously undiminished. In the end, we'll race because we want to, and we'll race, treasuring the wonder that we still can.

The weekend is approaching quickly. My throat is thick, and one ear hurts so much I can't bear to touch it. I shake my head and creek water swills around in it, searching for a way out. My left hip is higher than the right, but straightening my pelvis merely pulls my shoulder across. I'd hurt my back lugging Canadian canoes around on the holiday, and I'm still crooked. I know I won't be straight by the weekend, but I should at least be pain-free. I lie on the bed, legs elevated to let the blood drain out of the varicose veins so my legs look better than they feel. I form a plan of action: 1. Rest up as much as I can over the next few days to get on top of the ear infection, 2. Massage any residual stiffness out of the limbs, 3. Take the trusty back brace along just in case the internal scaffolding doesn't come right in time. All in all, I'm in good-to-go shape, and I should be even better by the weekend. I nod once to officially declare myself fit to ride, lie back and begin the long leisurely enjoyment of anticipation.

The race is being held at Kooralbyn resort, with the start/finish line adjacent to the resort buildings. Some of the soft competitors will have rooms booked, but not for us the temptations of decadent comfort. We intend to make do with an open-sided tent pitched in the temporary tent village that will spring up around the start. A tarp on the ground, a couple of folding chairs and a few eskies will be all we'll need.

In the background, I hear my wife, Joan, and Boyd's wife Mathilde talking on the phone about to change to the dynamics of the night.

"We're coming too," Joan announces. "We've booked a unit overnight."

"Brilliant," I respond with an instant shameless enthusiasm that betrays my true allegiances. I quickly claim the delights of their company as cause for my eager reaction, but it's the prospect of hot showers between laps and a soft bed on which to rest weary legs that's making me smile. Wives coming also means big, fully-packed eskies, cooked food, with thoughtful consideration given to all our needs, not just spare tubes for the bikes.

We make it down to Boyd's place before lunch. Over a ritual cappuccino, I ask Boyd what he's done about lights. I figure this will be a one-off affair, so I've bought a cheap light for the front of the bike that runs off AA batteries. I've also taped a small torch to my helmet for added illumination. They lit up the bedroom well enough, but I've a nagging suspicion they might prove somewhat short of requirements. My fears are soon confirmed. Boyd's chosen the spare-no-expense option, and his light is blindingly bright even in daylight. I ask hopefully after the phase of the moon this weekend, but Boyd shakes his head, commiserating with a 'brave-fool' sympathetic grimace as if I was proposing to climb Everest in bare feet.

It's been raining all week, and we dodge showers all the way out to the course. Grey curtains hang threateningly over the coast, but fortunately, the sky in front of us is a promising patchwork blue. Preparations are in full swing when we arrive. A tent city is being busily erected, and a buzz of pre-race anticipation fills the air. It's been wet, but a hot summer sun is rapidly drying out the ground. All manner of open-sided tents and marquees are appearing around the start area. While the ladies head off to find our unit, we find some space and lay claim. We erect our small shelter next to a young family. An organized husband and wife with two young children under five are well-ensconced, with all the comforts of home compressed into a few square metres. Only a well-polished bike propped up beside the toys indicates this is no holiday outing.

"Are you part of a team? I ask.

"Doing it solo," the father answers, nonchalantly.

Twelve hours, lap after lap, all through the night. I shake my head. Yet, I'm only less crazy by degrees.

Setting up doesn't take long, and it's still too hot to ride the ten-kilometre course, so we spend the afternoon lazing in the pool, saving energy and enjoying the slow build-up to tonight's adventure.

"There will be a lot of coming and going from our unit tonight," I warn one of the other unit residents. "But we'll do our best to keep the noise levels down."

"That's not a problem for me," she replies brightly. "I never go to bed early."

"No, I mean we'll be coming and going *all night long*." I emphasise the words, but she's looking blankly back at me. I try to find other words for the madness involved, but there are none.

"All night long," I repeat, only this time I hear myself, and now both of us share the same bemused look.

Late in the afternoon, Boyd and I gear up to ride a lap of the course. Fiddling with our bikes down by the start, we don't notice the black cloud creeping up from behind the hill and suddenly darkening the afternoon. In no time, we're huddling together under our open-sided tent, trying to stay dry as sheets of rain blow in horizontally. Small lakes form in the hollows of the roof threatening to collapse it. As the rain continues, it begins to run down off the hill, eventually forming a shallow river which flows ankle-deep across the start/finish line. The storm lasts for half an hour. The cloud eventually drifts on, the sun re-emerges, but it's now too low in the sky to effect any drying of the ground. Tonight there will be no sweet dirt smell in the air, and no hovering dust haze to sting the eyes.

The afternoon has nearly slipped away as we set off on our practice ride. The grassy ground is soft and yielding. It will only take a few sets of tyres to chop it up, and a few thousand sets to transform the carpet of fresh, washed green into a thick porridge of clawing brown mud. I tiptoe my spotless bike over the surface in a vain attempt to maintain its gleam, and a disturbing reality comes and whacks me on the back of the helmet. My modest mountain biking experience has never encompassed riding in the dark before, but in my brief history, I've also managed to avoid ever having to ride a bike through serious mud. It crosses my mind that the pitch black of night might not be the best time to learn the finer points of mud riding. A sobering apprehension begins to muscle aside my upbeat mood. We manage to make our way up and over the first few hills, with Boyd nearly as unsure as I am as we slither and slide over the muddy ground.

"Try and keep to the high side of the track, where the ground will be more solid," he counsels, after I yet again slide through a corner and lay the bike down in the mud. The practice ride comes to a bloody end when my foot slips from the pedal and the rotating pedal takes a chunk out of my shin. We slither our way back to the start, subdued, my leg running rivulets of brown and red, and I head off on a search for bandaids.

Roy hasn't yet arrived. He's coming straight from work, and as usual, he'll cut it fine. We occupy the remaining time fuelling up. There will be no need to watch what we're eating tonight, so we pile on the pasta. With a full fuel load on board and only half an hour to the start, I go looking for Roy amongst the crowd. Usually, he can be heard before he's seen, and I listen out for him above the music and the excited noise. I find him already at our tent. As usual, he's jumping out of his skin with barely suppressed excitement and as usual, his bike isn't quite ready to go. This time he has no working brakes. Unperturbed, he takes time to introduce me to Gus, the fourth member of our team tonight and then heads off on a frantic search for a good mechanic. I soon realise Gus is not just here to make up the numbers, Gus is the real thing. Short and stocky, he works away on his bike with tell-tale, practised efficiency. I suggest he might like to lead out while Roy gets his bike in working order and he takes the suggestion in his stride, merely increasing the pace at which he's working. We chat while he fixes a homemade, mud-resistant plastic contraption to the underside of his bike. Just as I have quickly summed him up, he's also rapidly worked me out and, taking pity, offers as much advice as he can compress into the few minutes available.

"Spray vegetable oil on all the under surfaces," he tells me. "That will stop too much mud sticking."

He talks quietly on, and I greedily take in the gold-like information he's giving out. But time is slipping away, and soon Gus has to head down to the start. I tell Boyd he'd better get himself organized to go second, and presuming Roy has his bike together, he can go third. Thus I can assume my rightful position, and head off last.

We start exactly at seven o'clock, as the last rays of light retreat behind the hill. Good-natured chaos ensues as the pack of wobbling bikes picks its way up a narrow chute and out onto the track proper. I spot Gus solidly muscling his way through the middle of the press of stray elbows. He's obviously not going to prove the weak link in this team. Roy reappears at the tent. His bike is together again, and with his great-to-be-around self, back to full volume. I confirm that he hasn't eaten, and tell him to relax, and that Boyd will go second. He's looking weary having rushed here after a day's hard yakka, so I take him to where a big pot of pasta and mince sits on the stove. As we wander over towards the unit, we stop to watch the magical lantern show make its way up the hill, string out into single file and snake its way across the slope. It's a unique, mesmerizing spectacle of dancing lights that demands we stop and watch. I'm thinking that if someone had suggested, a few years ago, that I'd be participating in something like this, I'd have asked them if they had rocks in their head.

"Thanks," I say, looking over towards Roy.

"Thanks for what?" he asks.

"Just thanks."

Roy slides broadside into the change area. He smells of mud and sweat. He slaps the all-important Velcro-backed number of the Daggs onto the front of my bike.

"Enjoy it," he says, and I'm off. Mud sucks at my tyres, but I still take off hard for the benefit of the little cheering crowd which sends me on my way. I lift my watch up towards the small torch on my helmet — 9 pm exactly. I clear the penumbra of lights surrounding the start and, more quickly than I'd expected, the pitch-black night envelopes me. I'm alone, with the impenetrable blackness broken only by a small rectangle of light a few metres across, focused five metres in front of me. Soon the silence also becomes total, with only the sound of my already-laboured breathing intruding into the quietness of the night. By habit, I lift my head to see the path ahead, but everything in front of me is black, and unknowable.

As I move uphill at just over walking pace, objects appear in an orderly slow procession. Then I reach the first one-eighty turn, and slip back downhill. Standing up on the pedals, I push my helmet up out of my eyes, blink furiously in nervous readiness, and steel myself for the roller-coaster ride ahead. Trees begin to leap out at me from the darkness, attracted it seems from miles around by the light. Cool wet mud sprays up my leg. Without any forewarning, the ground rises and falls alarmingly in front of me, and my fingertips hover permanently near the brakes. I'm soon feeling like a train running out of control, ready to wreck at any moment, but the feeling is also at the same time strangely exhilarating. It takes me no time to realise that Roy is right — this is going to be such a good way to spend a night, and much better than sleeping it away.

I quickly learn the rules of riding in the dark. Too much speed generally is bad but, simultaneously, I learn the different rules of riding through mud — speed is mostly always good. Survival's quiet voice quickly teaches me that flying into a ninety-degree corner before knowing whether the track turns right or left, has a limited future, while coasting quietly through deep mud will always have the same soft, sticky, wet outcome. I soon learn the absolute importance of keeping the front wheel straight whilst ploughing through mud, but applying the same principle when the path disappears in front of me leads to a more intimate bush experience than is desirable. It only takes a single lesson to understand that when a log leaps out of the darkness, I absolutely need to either brake hard or pedal hard, and that a steady-as-she-goes, hope-for-the-best approach can only end in tears.

My light and I both fall off twice during the first round. Neither of us is hurt, and I make it back in one mud-splattered piece. I look at my watch — forty-eight sweaty minutes, with time off for fixing lights and straightening bikes. I pull off the Velcro number and send Gus on his way. One lap down, and the prospect of a whole night of muddy fun ahead — next lap, I'll be ready to really go for it.

I hose down the bike and myself, and fall into the swimming pool. Joan and Mathilde are still awake, and I share a full basket of highlights with them. The rhythm of the night has now been established. Frantic full-bore effort, then cool down, shower, swim, relax, eat, socialize, and then ready myself for the next round. Roy and Gus are lapping in the high thirties, Boyd's in the low forties, and I'm in the high forties. I count out time on the clock face, and work out when I'm due out again. I also count out Roy's numbers, otherwise he's likely to still have his feet up when he should be down at the start.

Second time out, I'm much more relaxed, and wiser. The first round was a good teacher, and I've come to an accommodation with the lack of light. I've stopped lifting my head to see where I'm going, merely keeping my eyes fixed on the rectangle of light in front of me and dealing with whatever appears. Gus has told me to stay in a higher gear than I'd usually use, so I can power my way out of the mud and any other difficulty. The fast lap doesn't happen. My mud-encrusted chain starts to jam on every steep uphill, and I find myself walking hills even I would normally ride. But it's not all bad. A thumbnail moon is floating on its own partially illuminated cloud, and a twinkling smoky Milky Way whiteness of tightly bunched stars is arched across the pitch-black sky. I stop and make sure I take a few moments to enjoy the rewards of the still, magic, dead-of-night silence. Right now, I can't think of anywhere I'd rather be, or anything I'd rather be doing.

A log appears. I've been expecting it, and I've time to push down hard on the pedals. Beyond the log is a black void where the ground falls away, and I half expect I'll be bucked over the handlebars, but the front forks willingly forgive and I ride on, quietly ecstatic. All through the lap, a steady procession of riders with huge helmet-mounted searchlights come up behind me, and for the few minutes it takes to catch and pass me, the night is wonderfully illuminated. I feel sorry for them, as being able to see what's ahead surely can't be nearly as much fun as speeding down the highway with only your parking lights on.

Two laps down and it's not even midnight. Joan and Mathilde have become bored and gone to bed. I'm not even feeling remotely tired. I've got a bike to hose down and a chain to clean. The swimming pool is still looking inviting, and I'm hungry. By the time all that is attended to, it'll be nearly time to saddle up and do it all again.

Roy's good to talk to at any time, but even more so in the middle of the night. He's never been a straight-line thinker, but he's deep. The later in the night, the more right-angled his thinking becomes, and the deeper it gets.

"How's it been for you out there, tonight?" he asks me.

"I don't mind the mud," I say. "The hills are hard, though, with them being so slippery. Take a few of the longer hills out, and I'd be having a real ball."

"No," Roy says. "You've got to welcome hills, hills are good for you."

"Yeah, I know, I know," I say in easy agreement. "Hills are your friends, doing hills is what gets you fit."

"No, it's even better than that," he says, but quietly, his voice dropping as if he's about to let me in on a secret. "Doing hills makes you a better person."

"How's that?" I ask sceptically, unwilling to let him get away with woolly thinking.

He searches the ceiling for a few seconds as if looking for an answer. "It's all about the response, isn't it?" he says, pulling the idea carefully down from the roof, and handing it across to me with due reverence. "There are some really good things in human nature that are only brought out when hard stuff happens. And that's it, isn't it? You have to do hard stuff like riding big hills, or you never get the chance to make the right response." There's a wonder in his voice that's fresh, as if he, himself, has just newly seen this truth. "See, if you go through life and you don't have to face hard stuff, or if none of life's bad stuff ever happens to you, then lots of the good stuff never happens for you, either."

"So bad stuff is really good stuff?" I ask, in middle-of-the-night confusion and contrarincss.

"No, it's not that bad stuff is good, it's the response that's the good thing," he says, as if it should now be self-evidently clear to me. "It's no fun cleaning up after a flood, or dealing with the aftermath of fire, but even with the obviously bad, the response can make good come out of it."

He's obviously on a roll, and I nod with an almost understanding. The combination of fog and light he sees in my eyes encourages him to keep going.

"See, life isn't as hard for us as it was for lots of previous generations, and not as much bad stuff happens to us as happened to them — and that's all good. But the thing is, it shouldn't all be easy, and we all still need to be doing hard stuff, or we don't get this right response thing happening." He looks across at me to see if enlightenment has finally arrived, but I'm still struggling. "But get this. Where we're lucky is that we can often get to choose when to throw hills into our lives, and which hills we want to throw." He pulls at the sweat-matted hair on top of his head while the train of his thoughts accelerates towards its grand floodlit conclusion. "So the thing is we still absolutely need to do hills and welcome doing them, because if we don't do hard stuff, we miss a chance at becoming better people, simply because we never get the good response thing happening. You with me?"

He puts his hands behind his head in a way that indicates that surely we've made good progress, and then he sits suddenly forward and delivers things in real-time even as he's seeing them. "And would you believe it, it gets even better. It's not just us that get a chance to become better people." He pauses again for effect and I nod again, unwilling to interrupt the rapid thought train. "Everyone out there, tonight, is doing hard stuff, right?" he says with finger-pointing certainty.

"Right," I agree.

"And when people do hard stuff together, they don't just get a chance to be better themselves, they get a chance to get better together."

He's looking across at me making sure I'm following, when suddenly an image comes into my mind, of four of us riding abreast on the last steep section up to O'Reilly's in the Gold Coast Hinterland. I'm on the very inside, breathing hard and suffering badly. Boyd is outside me, but he has his hand on my back, pushing me along. Roy is outside him, with his hand on Boyd's back also pushing and outside Roy, Davy, with champion heart, and champion legs, is working the hardest, and pushing Roy up the hill, and all four of us are feeling good about the arrangement.

I nod, for suddenly I do clearly see what he's saying. "Out on the track, tonight," I tell him, "I never heard one single harsh word. Everyone is just so polite as they pass you — even when you're in their way. And if you've stopped, every single person, without exception, asks if you're OK."

"Exactly," he says, with both hands in the air to confirm the truth of it. "That's the good response thing I'm talking about. Everyone out there is doing the same hard stuff, and doing that hard stuff draws out the best in everyone. At the same time, it brings everyone closer together. Brilliant the way it works, isn't it?"

He drops his hands, and I sense we're done. Anyway, we are done for now. I point to the clock on the wall. "Boyd should be back in the next five minutes. It won't bring out the best in him if you're not down there."

He scrambles to find his helmet and shoes, then he looks across at me. "Does it get any better than this? Having fun, getting fit, doing hard stuff, becoming better people."

"No, it doesn't," I confirm, and he disappears into the darkness.

I wait at the start line, glancing nervously at my watch. Roy was due in five minutes ago. I count around the clock face again and confirm that he should be back.

Lights come in one by one — no Roy. Then, just as concern begins to really tighten my insides, suddenly he's skidding at me through the mud. We exchange the number.

"Handlebars got tangled up with a tree," he says. "Had to sit for a couple of minutes."

I give him a once over. "Are you hurt?" I ask.

He shakes his head. "Just winded."

Roy always bounces well, and I'll get the full story later. I stand up in the pedals, and once more head off into the night. I'd been thinking that at three in the morning, I'll be low in energy and sleepy, but I'm the opposite. The night has cooled off, and a light mist blankets the course, coating the grass with silvery droplets. I'm not even remotely tired as I power up the first hill. I even pass two people early on. I pass the first rider on a broad section of track, where I don't even need to yell "track right" as I slip past, but I do, anyway, just for the warm buzz this rare event gives me.

The later it gets, the more alive the bush seems to become. Frog noises now fill the muddy hollows, and an occasional spider drops to helmet height from the trees to see what's disturbing its peace. This will be my last lap in darkness. Gus has told me to keep in the middle cog all the way around to stop from developing chain suck issues due to the mud. Speed and night are a heady combination, and I start to have enough confidence to leave the brakes alone. I'm feeling good, and ready to rip the lap apart.

A set of lights comes up behind me. As I'm approaching a short steep rocky downhill section, I think of stopping to let him pass, but decide he can wait till we're through it. I bump my way down, aware his light, close up on my tail, is pushing me faster than I want to go. As with all these things, they happen quickly. All that I later recall is that one moment I am dropping down through the trees, and the next, the back wheel is coming up to meet my helmet, and I continue over the front of the bike. Somehow, survival instinct kicks in. I leapfrog over the top of the handlebars without becoming entangled, and make a running landing on the steeply falling track below while the bike continues to cartwheel past me. I turn to meet the threat of the closely following bike, but he's stopped high above me, his disembodied searchlight shining through the haze of dirt and debris the crash has thrown up. The searchlight firstly picks me out, standing like an Olympic gymnast who's just pulled off a triple somersault, but can't quite believe he landed on his feet. Then the light moves slowly on to the bike, its wheels still spinning. "Nice landing," the light compliments me, as it carefully steps its way down the rutted track and through the carnage. I ride the rest of the lap subdued, and much less inclined to tear anything apart.

Daylight arrives and instantly what was frightening turns tame and benign. Corners lose their ability to baffle and terrorise, trees return to being stationary obstructions. I now can raise my head and pick my line, and gears can be chosen early. On this round, I give myself permission to tourist along on the flat sections and suck in the experience. Below me, kangaroos are grazing on the dew-covered golf course. Above them, the timeless magnificence of Mt. Barney rises resplendent out of the mist. It's good to be up and about in the early morning. With the riding becoming disappointingly easy, I up the speed to compensate. If I can get around in the low forties and Gus can put in his customary fast lap, then Boyd will be able to squeeze in a final lap before the seven o'clock finish.

The bike and I have become a harmonious unit, and I keep the speed on, finally getting to gun the course. I ride at my limits, brushing trees with my shoulders and riding hard into the corners. I take on now-familiar foes, and go over the log without so much as a pause on the pedals. Much too soon, I'm turning out of the last one eighty-corner and as I do, I catch sight of a rider entering the same corner, fast. “No way,” I say as I flick up a gear, even though the track turns upwards. I travel the last five hundred metres out of the saddle, giving it everything I’ve got. It’s 6:15 a.m. on a lazy Sunday. I’m mud-splattered and completely happy. My thighs are burning, but my head is clear, and I know exactly what I’m thinking: ‘Doesn’t get much better than this, does it?’

CHAPTER 7
MUD AND OTHER DELIGHTS (EPIC 2)

I HAD TO THINK TWICE ABOUT INCLUDING SOME OF THESE stories and, in the event, I did remove some of the more extreme. After all, the premise of the book is that old age can be a fun time. I understand that some of these misadventures may not appear fun to everyone, and the last thing I want to do is turn you off. However, their inclusion does serve to demonstrate that, physiologically speaking, there are no insurmountable barriers for the aging body. With mountain biking, all that really happens is that it takes twice as long to climb the hills, though not that much longer to descend. The wonder of it all is that not only is the enjoyment just the same as when you were young, it is actually enhanced thanks to the realisation that this might not be possible for too many more years. It is, therefore, all the more precious.

In this chapter, I examine the proposition that exercise is medicine. Exercise is certainly medicine for the soul, but we also have to see it as medicine for the body. We have been sold the falsehood, that there is a pill which will fix each of our diseases. Drugs have their place, and in combating cardiovascular disease, we need all the help we can get, but exercise will cure more of what ails us than you might realise. We have to start seeing exercise not only as medicine, but as the first-line choice of medicines. It will come as no surprise that any organ in the body with an enhanced blood supply will do its job better. Being better perfused with nutrient-rich, life-giving blood just has to be of benefit to any organ. And of course, a better functioning pump and more and better pipes are the keys to that better supply.

Simply stated, exercise is the mechanism which triggers all sorts of good changes in the body. It is the natural and principal anti-inflammatory agent we have. It will deliver increased amounts of oxygen and nutrients to organs, which is a fundamental brick in the building of good health. It should also not escape your attention that the 'exercise pill' is free.

Bike riding might not be your activity of choice, but you should be able to find something that will raise your heart rate sufficiently, in a way that you enjoy. Sometimes that might mean a degree of perseverance. If you take up walking, for instance, knees and ankles might initially complain at the unaccustomed exercise. However, if you keep at it, many of those aches and pains might gradually disappear; because the body has a great capacity to make the kind of changes that deliver the joints and muscles you are now requiring. It might just take a little time for that to happen.

I hope that you are taking this message from the book: that perseverance with exercise is worth the effort. We simply don't ever get away with anything. There is a heart price, or reward, for each and every one of us depending on how we live our lives. Since heart disease is often symptom free until it is well advanced, the sooner we start, the better. Heart health is all about sowing, and reaping what you sow. Just as you will pay a price for inactivity, you will absolutely reap a reward for 'doing stuff'. Pay attention to heart health, and the reward you will reap will not just be longevity, but you will add quality of life to that longevity.

The Epic is one mountain bike event we still try to do every year. Being now well into our sixties, we now tend to only do the half version. When I was in my fifties, you could count on one hand the people over fifty who participated in the Epic, but when I now look at the competitor list, I find a few dozen riders in the over-sixty category. Things are slowly changing, and all around me, I now see an increasing number of older people out there 'doing stuff'.

Boyd rocks up late in search of a bed for the night. "Got a lunchtime BBQ up here on the Coast, tomorrow," he says, "but I put the bikes on the back, just in case you're up for a short ride, early."

"Short ride," I snort. "This weekend has got to be the big one, Boyd. Time's running out for us, and this weekend we need to find ourselves some big hills, and hit them hard. Really hard."

"No, you shouldn't be trashing yourself this weekend," he replies, looking at me oddly. "This weekend should just be a light workout. Nothing too strenuous."

"Nah, two weeks out we should put in a big one, and get the legs used to the idea of pain, then we taper," I insist.

Boyd's suddenly wearing a look of infinite pity, and for a moment I think he's about to put an arm around my shoulder. "The Epic's next weekend," he says with crushing gentleness.

"No," I say, rapidly doing numbers in my head. The last weekend in August — what's the date today? A terrible sinking feeling arrives with the answer.

"Peter B and I did a full Mt. Nebo last weekend, and then we finished it off with a couple of quick Mt. Cootha laps for good measure," Boyd says with annoying self-righteousness. "I did say come down and join us, remember?"

I'm remembering well enough — a lazy weekend on the couch in front of the TV.

"You've never, ever joined me for a Mt. Nebo, have you?" he points out.

"No," I confess, my head slowly bowing.

"And all those times, recently, that Roy and I have invited you on a Daisy Hill ride, you never once showed."

"I've had the flu lingering for a couple of weeks, now," I say, trying to mount a defence. "I've been getting back into things slowly, just riding to and from work."

"So, if I understand you right, your total training for the Epic has been riding to and from work, and a couple of weeks of that you've had off with the flu?" Boyd sums up.

Before I reply, I pull in my stomach, trying to hide the five kilos I've put on since last year's Epic, rather than the five I'd promised myself I'd take off. "It won't be a problem," I declare with more bravado than I feel. "With the drought and everything, the track will be fast and firm. We'll all motor along the creek, and I'll ease my way up and over the big hills. The legs will remember how to get to the finish."

By the next Tuesday, I'm watching an angry army of black clouds massing on the western horizon, gathering strength for a major assault on the coast, and by nightfall, the sound of heavy rain drumming on the roof accompanies me into restless dreams of exams about to be sat, with me yet to open a textbook.

The old Falcon's got four bikes on the back and one bike inside, sharing the cabin space with six of us. A heavy shower of rain, darkening the sky over on our left, sweeps across the Laidley area. Mathilde, doing her first half Epic, eyes it warily. The weather is everyone's preoccupation. Boyd's busy telling us tractor-swallowing tales about growing up on the black soil of the Darling Downs.

"But the course hasn't much black soil, that I remember," I declare confidently. "The first ten Ks or so are mainly gravel roads."

"No, There are significant black soil sections early on," Boyd responds firmly, with a country boy's confidence.

"We'll be right when we reach the creek, though, won't we?" I ask, suddenly overtaken by a disturbing vision of helmets slowly following back wheels down into a great, sucking, black soil morass.

"Upper parts of the creek are mostly black soil, too," Boyd confirms, and the car momentarily becomes silent.

Fighting a rising panic, I turn and try to pick Davy's champion's brain. "I brought along some heavily-knobbled downhill tyres, Davy, do you think I should put them on?"

"Won't matter," he replies.

"Why won't it matter?" I ask.

"Nothing will matter," he says in a faraway, resigned voice, as if our fates are sealed and tomorrow's carnage inevitable. "Whatever's on the bike, just go with it."

Still in annoyingly high spirits and knowing he's well prepared, Boyd is working on maximizing Roy's enjoyment of the coming day. "Roy, I reckon if you didn't feel you had to race every last person who tried to pass you, you'd get to the finish less trashed, and enjoy the day more."

Roy nods slowly, trying his best to come to grips with such a novel idea.

"Adopt my philosophy," Mathilde offers. "Start off slowly, then gradually ease back as you go."

"For some reason, they're sending the super masters off amongst the first groups this year," I point out. "So there will be a steady stream of bikes chasing up behind you, pushing you to go harder than is good for you."

"Just let them all go past?" Roy ponders out loud, trying on for size the foreign concept. We watch the struggle playing out behind his eyes, and then he laughs. "Exactly what I always intended to do this year. This years all about enjoying the ride," he declares, with an addict's sincerity.

Morning arrives; a weak sun is punching through the mist, promising an after-the-rain perfect, blue sky day. A much too casual breakfast and a pair of lost gloves, mean we're running late, and miss the start. Boyd and I ride straight down the hill and continue on through the start gate chasing the pack which is already disappearing over the first hill. Roy's still back at the car frantically turning out bags, searching for his ankle timer. We warm up on a few early undulations, then, an orange-clad Marshall stretches out a left arm and points me down a side track. "Welcome to the mud," he says with much too much relish for my liking. I return him a condescending look and a confident smile. Mud's like diving into that first wave on a cool morning swim; after the wet brown stuff sprays coldly up your leg there's a brief shock, and then it's all good. I'm not concerned about a bit of mud.

Boyd, of course, was wrong. And all those, who over the years, still suffer nightmares about that Epic will confirm it — there was no *black* soil down that track. Rather, it was a rich, dark chocolate brown colour. And it wasn't mud, but a substance, thicker, stickier, and infinitely more evil than mud could ever be. A cross between glue and mud, endless glud awaited us.

I come up fast onto a scene of total confusion and chaos. The whole pack seems stationary in front of me. At first, I grunt and power my way past those already stuck fast in the glud, but soon all passages through are blocked. I bounce off Boyd's Clydesdale frame, and soon I too am part of the groaning crowd pushing their bikes through a sticky sea of the thick clinging stuff. Each rotation of the tyre adds another thick layer of glud which builds relentlessly, till the frame scrapes the porridge-like substance sideways, and spreads it richly over the chain and derailleur mechanisms. I try to mount the bike again, but it's like trying to pedal while simultaneously pulling hard on both brakes. For a while sheer muscle power keeps the wheels turning, but eventually the legs fatigue, the wheels cease rotating, and glud wins out. The back wheel sticks solid and refuses to turn. Off the bike and sliding frozen wheels over the surface of the reluctantly parting mush adds layers of it to the shoes; I grow steadily taller and my feet heavier. All around me, people are searching for sticks to poke and scrape with. Life for everyone is reduced to putting ten kilometres of effort into riding a few hundred metres and then, when the back wheel no longer turns, stopping and scraping a few kilograms of the evil glud off before starting the process all over again.

I catch up with Boyd's friend Peter. I know he's super fit and well prepared. "What are you doing back here with the also-rans?" I ask.

"Still recovering from the flu," he croaks, offering me a pale smile.

"Should be under a hundred Ks left by now," I encourage him, as my bike grinds to a halt once more. I watch him cough his way off up the track, and as I search for one of the bent, thick-handled, thin-tipped sticks I've quickly come to favour, I wonder if he'll make it to the end this year.

Roy catches up while I'm busy scraping a few kilos from the bike's weight. True to his word, he's touristing along chatting merrily to whoever will engage him, and with his irrepressible enthusiasm, encouraging anyone who looks even remotely depressed by the conditions. We're momentarily onto gravel, and he stays with me for a while, talking tactics in dealing with glud.

"Less drama if you just keep riding," he advises. "It builds up so quickly, that scraping it off's just wasted effort."

The surface of the rolling gravel hills is solid, and these hills are no longer the hard part of the ride. Instead, they are mud-free friends. On these long, restful, gravel inclines, my pedals barely turn over as I give the legs a break. Roy, never pedestrian, is wobbling all over the place, as he rises to the challenge of staying with me. Glud has not even dented his enthusiasm for the day. He knows lots of people, and as we ride along, he enthusiastically introduces me to a succession of grim-faced souls who are as preoccupied as I am in simply keeping the bike upright and moving in a forward direction. Eventually, he grows bored with the pace, and decides he needs to ride forward to see how Boyd's coping. He charges off up the road and quickly disappears.

I was hoping Ma Ma creek would be different, but it offers no relief. There are no downhills steep enough for momentum to scrape the mud off, so all forward movement, including any downhills, is down to leg power. My glud-fouled chain has stuck in the middle cog, so I find myself walking the far side of every creek crossing, dragging the dead weight of the bike beside me. I'm moving along at a snail's pace, expending huge amounts of energy in just keeping the wheels turning. Thirst is becoming an issue, and the challenging novelty of riding through thick glud has long since ceased to be fun. I weigh the alternatives: sit down and cry or keep ploughing my way to more solid ground. I decide that crying will waste valuable water, so I keep going and, slowly but surely, the track begins to firm under wheel. I'm able to generate some pace. It only takes a few good rattling downhills, the black soil gloom lifts, and the day starts to be fun again.

Somewhere along the creek, the first contingent of the serious, head-down-bum-up pack suddenly sweeps past. "Go, Davy," I say, but I don't think he hears. In a few seconds, they disappear around a corner.

At the first checkpoint, I spend ten minutes chipping away at the drying glud until I succeed in getting the chain to throw across to the small chain ring. On the bottom slopes of the Razorback, it's still jumping everywhere but, eventually, it settles in a 'granny-enough' gear, and up I go.

Towards the top of the mountain, my legs call for a conference. They politely inform me they're switching to reserve energy supply. It's a message which, previously, I've usually had delivered climbing up into Edward's gap when a mere twenty kilometres from the finish, but today the whispering is starting while I'm still well short of halfway. Soberly, I consider my options. A good rest and a refuel, and my legs will knuckle down for a while. I know I can cajole another twenty or even thirty Ks out of them, but then it could get very ugly, as the whispering muscle fatigue turns to a long, continuous scream.

Tonight, there are sure to be some well-deserved recriminations over my lazy preparation. I haven't shown this ride the respect it demands, and I've paid the price. I watch the beauty of a thin line of moving colour slowly snaking its way up towards the summit. There's a cool breeze blowing, and the blue sky has an after-the-rain crispness to it. The views are spectacular. There could be much worse places to be, and greater disappointments to cope with. While I'm muddy and weary, I'm blessed and very lucky to be able, once again, to haul myself up to the top of the Razorback. It goes against the grain, but acceptance comes very quickly. After all, there is some attraction in being freshly-showered at the finish line, ready to dispense sympathy and understanding, rather than being the one prostrate on the ground unable to move another inch. Although I hold out a faint hope the flats will magically restore the legs, I make my decision and, once made, the day suddenly becomes extremely enjoyable. I wring out the maximum pleasure from whatever energy I have left.

Holding on for dear life as I try to survive the first steep downslope off the Razorback summit, I come across a unicycle dancing its way down the deeply-rutted slope. I'd often wondered how on earth a unicycle could possibly cope with such steep descents, but I now watch, up close, the impressive arm-flapping ballet that's needed to keep it upright. However, I'm in danger of doing some arm-flapping, over-the-handle-bars stuff of my own if I keep watching his efforts, so reluctantly I apologetically squeeze my way past.

In case the answers have changed, I ask the legs a few final questions coming over the loose rocks into checkpoint two. When I get their answer, I accept the verdict.

"Roy and Boyd left ages ago," my wife announces as I arrive. "They both seemed awfully tired, though."

"My legs have just about had enough," I say not looking her in the eye.

She gives me a sideways look as if she can't decide whether I've newly returned to sanity, or finally lost my mind. "What!" she exclaims, "you're quitting?"

"Withdrawing," I correct. "Tactical decision — just wouldn't get home in daylight." Feeling like a deserter, I quietly load the bike onto the back of the car and, keeping my eyes averted from the braver souls struggling on, take the long way round to the finish.

Mathilde is there, excited and glowing with the achievement of finishing her first half Epic adventure. Davy's there, too, shirtless and looking like he's just been on a short training ride around the block, his bike already cleaned up. Peter B makes it in, and I find him, pasty and triumphant, lying as near to the finish line as he could respectably fall. He can barely raise his head, and he hasn't stirred from the grass, but I recognize the look of exhausted satisfaction he wears. Boyd and Roy roar in together both looking much too fresh, and each with a different version of who waited for whom on the final run to the finish.

The ranks of finishers are notably thinner this year. The mud has made for a different and much harder day, but the sense of achievement on the faces of those who finally stumble over the line is all the more acute because of the conditions. The Epic wouldn't be the Epic if it weren't a challenge, and this year the course has won many of the contests waged against it. As usual, it's sorted out those who prepared well from the rest of us. And as for the rest of us … there's always next year.

CHAPTER 8
REVENGE

RECENTLY, I'VE BECOME AWARE OF THE INCREASING NUMBER OF studies which demonstrate how regular exercise benefits people suffering from all sorts of disease states, including people with dementia and those undergoing chemotherapy for cancer. I find studies like these interesting, and the results not unexpected. However, whenever I read a study that concludes that regular exercise will improve the cognitive performance of dementia patients, particularly those suffering vascular dementia, my reaction tends to be along the lines of, 'Why is this a subject of recent research?' Surely we should have worked out long ago that when all organs, including the brain, are better perfused with blood they function better. That these studies are only now being done, speaks to me more about our underlying fundamental views of old age and what we expect of the elderly. In the past, we have let the old, and particularly the very old, slip quietly into states of total inactivity, where bones become fragile and all muscles, including the heart, deteriorate. Then falls happen, hips fracture, people suffer strokes. The downward spiral accelerates till it becomes fixed, and irreversible. We let this happen because of the all-pervasive notion that the appropriate response to the increasing frailties of old age is rest and inactivity. In our nursing homes, sitting in a chair all day carries less risk of a fall than having people up and about strengthening their muscles, increasing bone density and better perfusing their brains. Worse still, those thought to be at risk of hip fractures are even put to bed and given padded pants to wear; this, of course, only increases their risk of fracture when they do get up. Though undoubtedly motivated by kindness and concern, much of how we treat the old only serves to accelerate their decline. In this pervasive mindset, old hearts are seen as fragile and not to be strained. It is precisely this attitude that causes the deteriorations we fear, and yet the penny still does not seem to drop.

The great thing with exercise is that it doesn't matter where the starting point is, the body and the heart will always try to respond positively and make the changes that will allow it to perform whatever task we set it. It doesn't matter if the goal is to walk with the aid of a wheelie-walker for a hundred metres, on the flat, without stopping, or whether it's to run a marathon. There are bodily responses which will help us achieve the goal, as long as we give the body a this-is-what-we-do-regularly message. Of course, as with all goals, once we reach them we can set others. Suddenly we find we are walking two hundred metres, then three hundred. Blood is a life-giver. Every muscle, every organ benefits from being better perfused, including the pump itself. At their root, many of our diseases and ailments are either diseases of inactivity or diseases made worse by inactivity. Exercise is the key element in ameliorating many of the inactivity-induced ailments of old age.

Last year was the first time I'd failed to complete the Epic, and I've been waiting a whole year for redemption. 'Good news,' the email announces, 'we've finally managed to do away with the boring, long dogleg of bitumen after checkpoint two. Instead, we're taking you on a shortcut up and over the ridge.'

Great, I think, more dirt to enjoy, less uninteresting bitumen and a shortened distance into the bargain. But before my mind has a chance to fully applaud its approval, my legs ask for a review. For a moment, I try to visualize the valley. Certainly, it has widened out by checkpoint two, but when I open out memory's edges, I still see substantial ridges flanking the valley floor. My legs would never express concern over a few extra kilometres of flat bitumen, but confronting two or three hundred more vertical metres of climbing is a different matter. It's not much in itself, but in a race that already has over two kilometres of vertical, there will be a domino effect, with the energy used to climb the new metres of vertical being the fuel usually reserved for other major climbs. I try to imagine the knock-on effects, as I'll now well and truly be into reserve supply pulling up the steep ascent to Laidley Gap. That will only leave the last scraps of energy I usually use to reach the finish, to power me up and over Edward's Gap. And if every ounce of energy is expended in summiting that Gap, how on earth will my hollow legs propel me the last ten Ks?

After last year's failure in the mud, I'm psychologically fragile and I can do without the thought that the course might be even more difficult this year. I try to concentrate on the positives. This year I'm treating the Epic with respect, and my preparation hasn't been bad, like last year. I had a good workout at the Boonah marathon and did a hard fifty Ks in the mud at Noosa, so my legs are more than halfway there. I tell Boyd about this year's extra vertical, and his response is predictable. He orders me down to Brisbane on the next two weekends for a couple of Mount Nebo rides to get the legs as good as we can with the limited time available.

Without trying, I even manage to ride the second Nebo under race conditions. I'm late leaving for Brisbane, so I skip breakfast. Then, in the let's-get-rolling rush, I forget to fill a water bottle. In no time I'm dehydrated and out of fuel. It's all good acclimatization for the Epic, though the pancakes and cream at the café on the top of the mountain rather spoil the deprivation. Peter B is with us. He lets slip that he's not doing the full Epic this year. We protest. He's much younger than we are, and super fit, so why should he get away with a mere fifty while we're saddling up for the full hundred? However, he's just done a big hundred at Noosa in wet and treacherous conditions, and he's been psychologically scarred by the experience. I know what mud can do to the psyche, so I don't press the point. My own response, though, to last year's mud-caked failure has always been clear and very simple—revenge at any cost.

However, I'm very aware there are limits to what determination alone can achieve, and if your legs run out of fuel, then small hills will turn into mountains and even gentle gradients will make you weep at the impossibility of climbing them. I've done enough work to give me a good chance of getting to the end, but I'm worried that extra ridge is a ridge too far.

The night before my very first Epic, I'd slept soundly. It was the deep sleep of the blissfully ignorant. With every subsequent Epic, I've tossed and turned my way through the night. Is the bike mechanically sound? How will the new forks with their lockout suspension perform on their first big outing? The chain's a bit old and stretched, should I have replaced it? Will I come off on one of the thousands of places it's possible to come to grief? My sleepless mind dredges up all the places where I nearly lost control last time. My last memory of the course was a nightmare of mud, so will those memories resurface, or will it return to being the magical ride it was previously?

Dawn comes, and we're all up with intent. Roy wants to eat a long and leisurely breakfast, and tell the stories he forgot to tell last night. We missed the start last year, so Boyd is watching the clock and maintaining Roy's focus. Like a well-oiled machine, bikes and helmets and gloves and shoes are all ticked off and loaded; munchies are secreted in pockets, water bottles filled. We arrive early enough to enjoy the countdown and the jolly atmosphere of the start.

I fully expect Roy and Boyd to take off on the first hill and do their own thing, leaving me to tourist along like I usually do, enjoying the early morning bush, and savouring how lucky I am to be able to spend a whole day riding. But a few kilometres in, and I'm wondering if I'm feeling extra good, or if a few Mt. Nebos have left me fitter than I usually am. We're still all together. Roy's cracking jokes and encouraging everyone within hearing range. They stay with me for the first ten Ks till we come to the first big hill, then I lose them. I half hope they'll wait at the top but they keep going, and so I do the creek by myself.

It only takes the first long descent into the creek for all the mud demons of last year to be exorcised. In the fast-flowing run, the 'as-good-as-it-gets' feeling comes to the enjoyable fore. The back end of the day is a long way off, and concerns of finishing drown in the weaving speed and excitement of the run along the creek, and the invincibility of fresh legs. I reach the long climb of the Razorback feeling good, and settle into the task.

Interesting conversations are always to be had at the summit. By this stage of the day, the field is widely spread and I'm left riding with my kind of people — the old and infirm and the marginal, all of whom pause at the very top for a breather and a look at the view. I stop and chat to one middle-aged person who is throwing anxious glances back down the hill.

"Waiting for my wife," he says. "She climbs at her own pace."

"Good on you," I say, genuinely impressed. "First time you've done the race?"

"First time," he confirms."

"I hope you both make it to the end."

"Done lots of preparation," he announces proudly, "so we're a good chance."

I wish him luck, and launch myself down the hill. The conversation has distracted me, and in the back of my mind, I know there was one thing I needed to do at the top but I have forgotten what it was. The descent is long and steep. I usually enjoy it, but today I appear to be bouncing around the ruts, barely in control. Two young guys pass and sensing, I'm barely under control, one advises me to sit further back in the seat. A woman comes up behind. I ask her if she wants to pass, and she takes the opportunity. She's not even young. Three-quarters of the way down, I realise my problem. I've locked out the front forks, and I've been descending sans suspension. What a waste of a good downhill run, I think, but at least now I can feel less bad about having to let people pass me on a descent.

The middle-aged couple catches up with me on the final climb before the fast descent of the Devil's Tail. Suddenly a sense of disquiet passes over me, and I know I need to work hard and catch the wife just before the descent becomes too steep. I ride hard for a few hundred metres, till I catch up.

"You have to watch it down the bottom where it transitions from hardtop to dirt," I pant. "The gravel is often very loose."

I let the brakes go, and enjoy the fast descent. Down at the bottom of the hill, I forget my own advice and feel the back wheel start to wander alarmingly as I transition to the loose gravel. I steal a glance at a small group of people gathered on the side of the road. They are busy cleaning up a very sorry and bloodied rider who obviously hadn't held it together at the transition. I ease on the brakes as much as I dare and pass the husband who has slowed and is looking anxiously back up the hill. I brush off a bit more speed, swivel on the seat and see his wife has made it safely down.

The half way point is at a working farm, and just as I'm about to do a loop around the back of a barn, I catch sight of Boyd, looking very much as if he's saddling up, about to set off again. It's been four hours since I last set eyes on him. Fortunately, he also looks across, and sees me arriving. We swap stories, and I quickly refill the water bottles, have something to eat, then we're off again.

The new ridge is steeper than I'd allowed and rocky into the bargain, but I'm momentarily feeling refuelled and energized. That's the nature of a day like today. Sometimes a second wind will kick in, and then a third and a fourth, with periods of increasing weariness interspersed. I climb the energy-sucking, leg-wrecking ridge, almost daring to believe that the better preparation and back-to-back Mt. Nebos, will get me there this year. We survive some loose and rocky descents then we're safely over into the next valley, ready for a long drag up the valley floor. I tuck in behind Boyd, preparing to eat up the kilometres. Looking very strong, the married couple rides past. They'll make it to the finish, no sweat. Boyd is great to ride behind. One of the reasons I was so pleased to see him still at the halfway, was not just the companionship of riding with him, but the way he can ride in front all day on the flat, setting a relentless, even pace.

Soon we've a whole line of tiring riders tucked in behind us, taking advantage. I'm riding right at my limit, but I know this is so much better than falling off the back. Then my second toe starts to burn. At first, it is only low-level discomfort, but it soon develops into an I-can't-think-of-anything-else, all-consuming preoccupation. I don't know what will cause me to stop first — the toe or the redlining of my breathing. In the end, both call a halt together, and I ask Boyd to stop under the next big tree.

I've reached the transition which always arrives at some point in these events. Up until now, it's all been fun, but from now on the major preoccupation will be about surviving and making it to the finish. My neck is beginning to hurt, and my back to stiffen. My hands are taking turns at being numb. The sun is still hot, and as the hours and the kilometres slip by, extreme enjoyment is stepping aside. The less pleasant, but ultimately more rewarding elements of challenge, begin to take over. Boyd starts to draw away on the hills, and I have to let him go. Soon we reach the unrideable steepness of the climb up to Laidley Gap. The extra ridge is beginning to tell on my legs, and the sun is beating down uncomfortably hot on my bent exposed back. I can feel my heart trying to exit my chest, but one foot in front of the other will always get you there, eventually.

Boyd takes off on the descent before I quite reach the top. This is a fast, semi-technical descent, and the great thing about having a heavy fifteen-kilogram bike is that there is nothing twitchy about the way it descends. Nothing knocks it off line, and if the front wheel momentarily leaves solid ground, the weight will drop it back immediately onto terra firma. Compared to its feather-light ten-kilogram carbon brothers, which might fly up hills but are skittish on the down, my bike descends quickly and safely. I soon catch Boyd up, and continue past. At the bottom of the descent, I keep going. It will do his soul good to chase me for a while, and it takes several kilometres till he finally pulls up beside me.

Psychologically, the third checkpoint is a good point to reach. My body is saying it's had enough for the day, but my mind can now point out there are only a few dozen kilometres remaining, and overrule. We don't stay long. The focus has shifted to simply making it home. I don't know how I'm looking, but it must be bad, as Boyd keeps on asking me how I'm feeling. We start to go through highs and lows. I know it would be fatal to stop for any length of time, so we have mini breaks. These are the short, 'have a drink, refocus and keep going', type breaks.

"Always a bit more hill than you think," Boyd says, reading my thoughts.

Yet in all the pain, there is still enjoyment. After a whole day on the bike, I'm in tune with the machine, almost indestructible and entirely careless. It's as if I can't fall off. I begin to let the bike career down hills with complete abandon, trying to get as much run up the other side as I can. I'm walking most hills, now, not just the big ones. Boyd is mostly still riding, and has to wait longer and longer at the top of each hill for me. We're back onto single track, climbing a long hill. At the top, a helpful marshal tells us it's only eight Ks to go. I'm ready for this information, though. I could have sworn we've travelled five kilometres since the last cheery soul told us it was only ten to go, but I've done this race before. The rider struggling with us, however, is close to tears at the news. I think he's about to sit down and perhaps never get up, so I quickly tell him, as an old hand at this particular strange exhaustion, that we're about to encounter some long, downhill single track, and the next few kilometres will pass very quickly.

I know I'm in a peak when Boyd wants to rest, but I want to go on and get this thing done. I start to play a game with myself. Four kilometres to go, I calculate, but immediately disbelieve myself and add another two to correct the number to the likely real-world distance. At times I feel like we're indulging in pure mountain biking; at one with the bike, weaving across the landscape, held on the endless ribbon of track by an unseen string. Even with wish-time adjusted to real-time, I sense we must be getting near. Boyd stops to field a 'where are you' call on his mobile, and motions for me to keep going. I can almost smell the finish. Then I receive confirmation as the sounds of a large gathering of people begin to float towards me on the breeze. I've had my revenge, I've made it. My hands relax their grip, and I set myself to enjoy the last few hundred-metre run in to the finish. Then, without warning, something pitches me forward over the handlebars. The bike ends up vertical, propped up against a tree, my legs still entangled in the frame. I look to try and find what has tripped me up, but there is hardly a single root or rock to be seen. Two riders ask through weary masks if I'm hurt. "Only pride," I reply. I've ridden all day without a single incident, only to be tossed over the handlebars by weariness and a single two-inch rock, not a hundred metres from the finish. Boyd catches up with me, and we ride along the fence, my knee stinging and about to stiffen, and receive a hand-slapping reward from Roy and various other family and friends. I know the eye-watering pain in my knee that accompanies me over the line will quickly recede, and the weariness that will replace it will be a good one. I've had my revenge on the course, but as usual, it's had the last laugh. I'll stay weary for a few days then the weariness will go, and I'll feel just that little bit stronger than I was before the race; the body healthier. Life's like that — you reap what you sow, and revenge can be sweet — painfully sweet.

CHAPTER 9
CANCER AND BROKEN BONES

One of the most obvious objections to older bodies undertaking high-intensity exercise, and one of the greatest hurdles, is that bodies become worn out with age. There is a good argument that regular exercise can help slow, and even reverse, some of the natural wear and tear processes. Nevertheless, pain or loss of capacity might be expected to accompany exercise as we age. We probably experience two types of pain. The first is merely overuse pain, which will resolve with or even without rest, and can be managed or ignored. The second is the pain from the body actually wearing out. Our joints have often lost cartilage, discs protrude, and old injuries come back to bite. Roy is a good study in this. Roy rode motorbikes in his youth. He always rode faster than anyone else and as a result had multiple, bone-breaking, joint-disrupting accidents, the last one of which was a big one he was not expected to survive. The consequences revisit him often, and it's not unusual to catch a grimace or a groan accompanying some particular movement. However, in Roy's pleasure/pain equation, where the pleasure gained from 'out there' activities is weighed against the pain experienced in doing the activity, he finds extreme pleasure in what he does, and the pain sitting on the other end of the scales seems light in comparison.

With all of us, there certainly may be more niggly pain and discomfort associated with exercise as we age. But the operative principle that nonetheless applies to the discomforts of aging is that exercise will generally improve things and inactivity will make things worse. Now that we're all well into our sixties, those of us with good joints have not eased back in the slightest. We all reached sixty fitter than we were at fifty. However, Roy last year became quieter on our rides, and less voluble. During one day-long ride back to my place, he inexplicably was dropped on the last hill, and pulled up limping and quiet. It was apparent to us that the pain/pleasure scales had suddenly tipped the other way. One month later, Roy had a total hip replacement.

Of course, it hasn't slowed him down in the slightest. Now pain-free, he's just about totally out of control. We almost succeeded in keeping him off the bike until his hip healed, but it was hard work. His excuse was, "I asked my surgeon, and he agreed bike riding would be good for my recovery." Eventually, Roy did accept the argument that hurtling down, steep, single track trying to beat your best time a few months after having a hip replaced, was not what the surgeon understood by bicycle riding. Luckily, anytime he did come off, he contrived to not land on his healing new hip.

Roy's attitude might be extreme, but in this case the extreme informs the ordinary and the commonplace. It is our attitude to the developing infirmities of old age, which becomes important. It is the 'what will this still let me do?' question we should be asking rather than easy acceptance of what we can't do. If we persevere, we might find our pains recede, and we slowly push back the boundaries of what we thought was possible.

I knew that I had to be especially vigilant with Roy at the time of his new hip, and made many phone calls gently arguing the case as to why it was a bad idea to be riding his mountain bike so soon after the hip replacement. I worked hard to keep him off the bike till everything had healed properly, because he had well established form with these things.

"What do you reckon?" I ask Boyd. "Do you think I should see if he's well enough to do the Noosa ride this year?"

"How long have we got before that one comes around?" Boyd asks in return.

"It's still seven weeks away."

"And if we add two weeks to that …"

"Nearer three weeks," I correct.

"I think he might, you know. That would be close enough to three full months."

"We'd have to do the easy fifty, of course," I point out, knowing Boyd was set on doing the hard fifty this year, having missed last year due to a family wedding.

"I'd rather do the easy fifty with Roy on board, than the hard fifty without him," Boyd replies with instant solidarity.

I'd tentatively pencilled in this ride as Roy's comeback event, ever since we found out he had prostate cancer and would require major surgery. I had a fantasy that perhaps I could nurse him around the course — even push him up the odd hill as required, as he had done for me so many times. After all, it doesn't take long to lose condition after a long lay-off.

I ring him up and put the proposition to him. "Why wouldn't I?" he says. "That's one of the best rides around. In a couple of months, I'll be completely back to normal."

"A big operation like that will knock you about more than you realise," I caution.

"Nah," he says, dismissing the suggestion. "I'm good again, already. It's more about when I can sit on a bike seat."

"I've got a big wide one you can have if you want."

"Thanks, I might try that. I'll pick it up on the weekend. We're still good for the weekend, aren't we?"

Knowing Roy would be finding it hard doing nothing, I've invited him up for a rest and recuperation weekend.

"Yep, the Mary River's still in flood. There will only be a few little rapids to negotiate, so as long as you're up to sitting in a canoe for a few hours, and promise not to fall out, I thought we might go for a paddle."

"I'll bring the bike too," Roy says quickly, before I have a chance to object. "We can go for a ride in the morning, and load up the canoes after lunch."

I take in a breath through my gritted teeth, and try to be gently diplomatic. "Two weeks after a big operation, you can tear things. You just shouldn't be anywhere near a bike seat for a long, long, time yet.

"Don't need to sit — I'll stay off the seat all the way. It will be nearly three weeks anyway, and things should be pretty well glued back together by then."

I try and compromise. "There are some good flat trails around the dam, and maybe …"

"No," Roy interrupts, "flat's no good to me. We need to do hills. That way I'll either be up off the seat, climbing, or off the seat, descending. If we do big enough hills, I won't ever have to sit down."

We all went for a long ride the day before Roy's operation, thinking that would be the last Daggs outing for many months. Now, not three weeks after the surgery, I watch Roy climb a hill that Boyd and I have long since given away. I now accept that the fantasy of pushing him up the hills in the coming event was always an illusion. We won't be doing the easy fifty, either. It will be hills, hills, and more hills for us again this year.

More disasters! It's turning out to be a frustrating year for the Daggs. Boyd's gone for a walk across East Timor, and taken a tumble with a fully laden pack. The result is a nasty ankle fracture running down into the joint surface. We had a whole series of events pencilled in this year and, frustratingly, he'll miss them all.

It's only a few weeks after the accident, but Boyd and his plastered leg still front up for the Noosa event as his wife Mathilde is doing the easy fifty, and is showing one of my daughters the ropes in her very first mountain bike event. Roy and I are taking on the hard and hilly fifty.

The night before the ride, Boyd picks up that Roy is quiet — too quiet. Missing is the usual 'let's get out there and have a fun day,' enthusiasm. Instead, there's a serious, focused quietness about him.

"He's looking to get out there and rip the course apart," Boyd predicts.

I hope Boyd's wrong, as I'd much rather it was like last year when I punctured only a few kilometres in, and Roy and I ended up right at the back. Then we stopped for an injured rider who'd come off and smashed an elbow, and Roy helped co-ordinate the efforts to get him out of the bush, to a place where an ambulance could pick him up. With us way behind, Roy was content to ride with me, catching up with stragglers, encouraging every one of them in his inimitable way, and frequently expressing to me how great it was to be simply out here doing this kind of stuff.

However, Boyd proves to be spot on. This year, Roy lines up early with the young guys, good to go when the hooter sounds. I have to point out to him that the vintage riders are the last wave to leave. Even then, he edges his way towards the front.

"I thought our place was always at the back," I joke, sighing desperately.

My vision of a leisurely four hours of enjoyment has ended in Roy's fixed stare. By the first corner, he's already yelling back at me, "Stay with me," and I have to politely ease my way through the massed bikes to get on his wheel. "I'm on," I say for the first of many times in the next ten kilometres, as we head out on the first section of single track. I like following Roy. He always takes the fastest line, while I always take the safest. Following him takes me way out of my comfort zone, and ups the excitement factor. It's undulating country, which gives me the best opportunity to keep up. I had hoped the forced layoff would have dented his fitness and I'd be somewhere near his pace, but it is a forlorn hope. I'm doing my very best, but I sense Roy is torn. He feels an obligation to stay with me, but as his true opposition disappears up the track, his cries of, "Are you on, yet?" after each hill, are becoming ever more desperately plaintive.

After the first mad ten kilometres, we start on a climb, and I get talking to someone riding a single-speed bike. My attention distracted, I fall back. Roy turns around towards me about to say something, thinks better of it, then I see a lift of his shoulders and he takes off at speed up the hill. Inadvertently, I've done him a favour. He's a long way behind where he should be, and he'll be able to reel in a long succession of riders over the next forty kilometres. He'll sight them in the distance, slowly catch up and, if they're up for it, duel for a while until finally subduing them. Roy loves to race, and today he's feeling strong the gift of life and health. He's been given a reprieve, so today he's out there celebrating for all he's worth.

On the other hand, having gone out much faster than my lungs were good for, I endure the opposite. I'm at ease with just plodding along enjoying the privilege of being able to climb hills on a mountain bike. I slowly drift back through the field, enjoying conversations and even dispensing advice in my areas of expertise. "Always try and stay on the bike," I counsel someone that I've slowly crept up on over a long, tedious climb, and who is now walking. "You'll find you'll use less energy if you stay on than if you walk. A hill like this is eminently doable if you practise riding very, very slowly." I stop beside a rider with shiny clusters that speak of a first outing bike and scratch my chin. As he pokes and pulls, I offer the opinion that a derailleur bent at right angles into the spokes like that is usually a terminal state of affairs. Offering appropriate commiserations, I ride on.

I'm walking the final steep pinch of a long hill when the first of the hundred-K riders comes past. I cheer him on and tell him how strong he's looking, but his appearance makes me remount the bike. Davy is doing the hundred this year, and I don't want to be caught walking when he passes. As it happens, I'm over the top, stopped by the side of the track trying to help a rider with a flat tyre, and the wrong kind of pump, when Davy comes scooting past.

He half props and turns in the saddle, with time only to ask, "You OK?" and for me to reply, "Yes, all good," before he disappears, bouncing and weaving at breakneck speed, down into the trees.

Last year the event was wet and muddy, and last night's sleepless thoughts were of last year's demons. I'm looking out for the short steep hill where I was concentrating so hard on bouncing down a series of wooden steps, that I forgot to turn right through the gate at the bottom, and ended up over the handlebars. The face plant was executed in a dramatic enough way for Roy to be shouting, "Speak to me, speak to me," until I came up laughing. This year, I come bouncing down the hill, and I'm easily through the gate and back on the track before I'm even aware that this is the same place. A couple of steep downhill switchbacks that last year spooked me enough so that I baled and walked, I ride this year while casually conversing with the person behind about how far we are from the next town.

I stop on top of the last of the big grassy hills, and reflect on how far I've come. I won't be last in today — not by a long way. The hills don't really hurt me badly any more, or take away from the enjoyment, and I've only really stopped at the top to breathe in the view. I recall conversations with Roy that at the time seemed far-fetched, fabulous pipe dreams. Yet each year since I turned fifty, we have become fitter than the year before, and if anything we're doing more stuff than ever before.

On the way to the finish, a young rider eases up beside me. I reckon he's had me in his sights for a few kilometres. He tells me he's had two punctures, and I understand why he's ended up behind. After a pause, he starts to wind up the pace and move ahead, but I've had such a good day, and in a way that Roy would be proud of, I stand up on the pedals and ride hard for home from a long way out. As Roy would say, "It's so good to be old, and still kicking butt."

Roy's at the finish, looking fresh, as if he'd like to go around again. Mathilde and my daughter are home in one piece, full of the joyful achievement of completing the ride. We all sit on the grass in the warm sun, spitting watermelon seeds, relaxing.

"You know what?" Roy asks rhetorically. "I think we'll still be doing this sort of stuff when we're seventy." He doesn't say it as a statement of intent, or even a goal, but rather as a just-this-moment-discovered glorious truth and is sharing it with us all. "Imagine that."

Nobody jumps in to contradict him, and I'm not even thinking to contradict him. Even Boyd, who has overdone the walking in his plaster and is stoically ignoring the pain, still manages to wear a believer's assured look.

"Boyd, of course," Roy continues, aware of his role in ensuring things happen, "is going to have to do a lot of swimming to maintain condition, and then a lot of running to strengthen that ankle once it's healed. I was talking to Mathilde, and she thinks we should all have a go at some triathlons next year. You can do off-road ones that involve mountain biking," he adds quickly, catching my reaction.

"Yeah, you all should," I say. "You'd all enjoy doing that sort of thing."

"We were thinking it was something we could all do," Boyd says in his 'I strongly recommend' voice.

"Well, I would," I say, "it's just a pity I can hardly swim, and I don't run because of my back."

Roy smiles, puts a hand on my shoulder, and a 'here-we-go-again' shiver runs through me. "This is something we all absolutely need to do ..."

ENDINGS

I'M HOLDING STATION IN A LONG LINE OF RIDERS THREADING A rapid descent of the wooded hillside. We're giving back a thousand feet of hard-won vertical in a matter of minutes. Fast falling on the slender edge of misadventure, I weave down through the trees, dropping wide-eyed over roots and rocks, hugging tight the dusty crumbling track. The protective instincts of consequence clamp my hands tightly to the handlebars, while the wild delight of untamed speed holds the rest of me loose and tingling. Before and behind, the hot complaints of tortured brakes become louder and more strident, the metallic smell of scorched brake pads mix with the sweet wood smell of the bush. From somewhere off to the side, an unseen marshal leaves a shouted warning of 'rock garden ahead' hanging in the air behind me, as the careless descent continues, unabated.

Yet despite all the speed and jolting fury, behind my eyes there is a stillness; a detached but intense living-in-the-moment joy-coated serenity that savours each mesmerizing tree-lined curve, bump and gravity-induced challenge the track throws my way. It's into this heady, rich, how-lucky-am-I thankfulness that something else intrudes. In that moment, I finally grasp where choice has taken me. A long journey embarked on in trepidation and hope has landed me in a good place, and I fully appreciate how much different my life might have been, from how it now is.

And that's the truth of it. We will all make choices as to how we age, and not all those choices will be equal in outcome. I hope you now understand more clearly how artery disease and heart muscle deterioration occurs, and how exercise is of vital importance in preventing and reversing those changes. I hope that, armed with the motivation that knowledge brings, you will make the choice to do more and not less as you age. That you will no longer see exercise as merely an optional lifestyle choice, but an essential part of extending and enhancing the quality of your life. Feel free to shake your head at one man's vision of growing old, and say, 'Not for me,' but the challenge set out here is to fashion options that are appropriate for you. The good news is that it is rarely, ever, too late. No matter what the state of current disrepair, our bodies are designed and programmed to respond to work, and to repair damage.

I do hope I've also presented the case for growing old *disgracefully*, where the vision of old age is active and fun-filled. As Roy might say, "Listen, you all need to do this! Health and happiness will be totally enhanced if you get out there doing stuff, and the more stuff, the better."

I for one am glad I made that fateful decision to go riding with Roy.

APPENDIX

OLD AGE REFUSE

And then came the days of slow repair
Of pale paper skin and wispy grey hair
Of light and dizzy trouble tossed sleep
Of cold white toes and sores that weep

How quick does fading yellow frosted sight
Dim a world once treasured crisp and bright
And ground which once was peacock strode
Become a fearful stumbling pot holed road

Every day we choose from our fine menu of pain
As worn aching joints and stiff muscles complain
We sigh and we trudge on life's slow weary way
Till with lament and regret the unerring piper pay

But insistent then we hear a soft dissenting voice
Assuring all we shuffling old we still have choice
That slow decline is not our fixed and lasting fate
The sublime rewards of change can equally await

So with our futures neither tethered sure nor fast
As alive to each new dawn as to our sunsets past
We don our helmet gloves and our cleated shoes
And paid in grateful joyous health old age refuse

ALSO BY SINCLAIR CURRIE

Knoblies (2018) Vanguard Press

(Pegasus Elliot Mackenzie publishers)

Broken Heads (2019) Vanguard Press

(Pegasus Elliot Mackenzie publishers)